I0I05007

TIME ENCAPSULATION 2010 Jan. 1st

I am First Viewer 5th D, a Remote Viewer, 2 years Military training, and over 3 years Iraq and Afghanistan. I assist with tips for the Law and the Military as well as Rescue. I have many accomplished views, I am also credited with the advisement of the covers they put up over the vehicles during the War in Iraq, early 2006 and recently the Nato/coalition testing of a laser device to go ahead of the vehicles to detect buried IED explosives. Awaiting lasers and teleports too….

The 'we' mentioned here is to the Bleeped Remote Viewer that 1st 5th is Psi Linked to. The Pentagon calls the Psi link 'Silent Talk'. Psi link is an ultra modern form of communication, using mental telepathy with a computer link in real time. Sometimes RNM can be used abusively, as on Court record; it is currently under investigation. Viewing is a Quantum 5th adventure, using Psi link (RNM) as we hyper shift along trails to the Stars.   site: www.nuts4mars.com

Open Stargate is not *about* Remote Viewing, it *is* RV writing & painting…this one opens in full running progress…

Remote View: Amazon Blow Gun Dart (in white dots); Crystal Skull; Conquistador's helmet
Remote View links to adventure movie 'The Kingdom of the Crystal Skull' starring Harrison Ford

Endorsed by: California Governor Arnold Schwarzenegger for the Views of his 'Predator' and 'Terminator' and 'Commando' movies

'Wow, Stargate gave Nasa the BOOT!'

29 July 2009- I won't have anything to do with them. Trashing a perfectly good Stargate. They've just got themselves *flushed*. Note to the skeptics - you're on your own. I refuse to listen anymore. They're relentless, they milk words, sounds, colors, people- the works. Anything and everything to upset and obfuscate. All designed to tear down our freedom to explore Stargate. I can't take it anymore. Extreme just about covers it. Open Stargate needs some serious upgrading. Reading my script? What for? It's been said over and over…the proof is there. No point to beating up on the warning system. That's pretty much what really preoccupies the Stargate Viewers, psi linked together and riding out the Time Tunnel. It is this psi link we use, others too I might point out, that is now (again, the ones doing it were clipped in Court once before by JAG Navy law, over abuse) once more abusing the RNM, or Remote Neural Monitoring. I prefer to call it just regular old psi link or maybe a fancy psi cast like David Brin the author. We will need to at the very least, now it is being abused, we need to make it essential to get the present operators the bleep away from it. Not sure if you can.. (A few extreme rants just got censored by myself there)… tribulations to come over the 'Swine Flew'. *With the RNM (that's Remote Neural Monitoring don't forget, being abused by CIA with ulterior motives and directives harmful to the security of our side,* for those of you who missed 'Remote Viewing: RAW') gone. We need the RNM abusers and abuse gone. Make no mistake about it. A very sinister threat to our freedom. Our side, our lands, our civilization. The yes, as in presently influenced, on the nano sly by modern psi computer enhanced applications being turned on unsuspecting citizens. Well, the RNM subliminal suggestions being transmitted no really, by the RNM digital boost they are currently using. With the super ramped RNM gone, those currently under its 'spell' will then and only then not be high risk to be sent out to do harm to our side, and hence become our enemy. But, that's about all I can suggest. We are right now at the hands of mad murderous

soulless Megs, giant prehistoric sharks, class A predators on the fear list, down below. Down below, as in Deep Black Secret Ops is where the Stargate is secured. Now, bringing this up to the surface, as fast as I can manage, bends and all.

Sharks tooth; it's a psi trained talent, the Viewer paints and afterwards sees the object.

If I didn't already have so many copies of it all in inert form, I would shut down the pc. Like the marriage theme white as in pure they are attempting to use for Sharia 'suasion, like the 'alters' for weddings, they are now playing off that term, and altering evidence. On personal computers, digitally going into the computer not just online. They go in and take out whatever bothers them and would hang them. They are altering our files, not my personal computers, like mine, they went into the Canadian Health departmental files, hacked. I already learned from that one, now I have hard copy and back up digital files on a redundant. Trust no one and back up your back up. You're going to need it. Nasa is up, in orbit around the Earth, and it was the Nasa claim they wiped out and I had to find a copy to retrieve it. Cheapo Terrorism 101. Main priority these days is focusing on getting those RNM centers in friendly control and get the psi link now turned into an abuse weapon, stopped. My suggestion is to remove the RNM heads in there as temporarily incapacitated victims of a vicious RNM attack on sensibility. Then reinsert some of our normal established law and order. Do it quick the head noise at the top is leaking. Not making sense anymore. I say, pick a day, any day. It has been done before. Something happens, men respond, good old Earth eh. Just takes resolve, strength and SWAT. Remove them you don't have to kill them. Just round up. They are starting to show sides. The torture experiment came out of Stanford University, USA. Get our side's forces happening and you will find so many others ready to bail and just waiting for it to start. The ones not under RNM. We just need to get the old ball rolling like in the 'Raiders of the Lost Ark' movie. So we commoners can at least prepare ourselves. There are other victims of the assault weapon. Bleep and I are immunes. There are of course others taken for other reasons. Don't let the ghouls eat the immunes. I think the RNM abuse on unsuspecting citizens is creating ghouls of a sort. They are driven, and would not be doing the things they are doing so mindlessly and uninformed, if they were not sent out to. Horribly enough, right now they are the exception not the norm. we can't let it cross over into the norm not the exception or we are doomed…Act sooner not later, in the interests of our freedom and survival. Nothing less than. Pick a day for Day One for our side, the clear winner. The cops could try now, use untouchable's rules. Go for it. They could, but I don't think they will. They have the Military over them. They can team with the Military and both act, like the regular means of fighting and doing counter to the Terrorists plans. Play their cards. I am getting a passport. I refuse to stay and watch you all go mo if it doesn't get fixed. Australia maybe…

fine. They can do their trip in the fall I am not remotely interested in watching them …as an Immune it would be sickening to me. That's all that's left. These others are under their spell; we all don't want to be here when ghouls set the new normal. So, into the Light with them!

They hired Leon Panetta as Chief of the New Get Smart, the CIA because of the Lion Shayk Osama bin Laden and the ancient Egyptian Sphinx pointed to Leo the Lion constellation, in 10,000 BC. Am I joking? Sadly, no. Nasa are stubbornly perceiving Stargate as if they place controls on this Quantum Ark-esque and make it theirs. Like trying to force God, or overpower goodness. I think there are likely hard drug users mixed in. They are using the needle. Well it makes you wonder. Listen to them, not even open to Quantum. Could be a side effect of the ninnies using RNM on them and subliminal reinforcements, and media cues to aid in their old fashioned pavlovian conditioning. Where the shrinks' experimenters used dogs and conditioned them to respond by simple continual repetition, until some pattern that was absorbed and 'learned' or overlaid on their own system. So that they responded correctly. Good thing humans are not animals and we have discernment capabilities.

View themed Door, insert carving Naqsh-e-Rostam, Iran ; large door View theme visual
match Afghan.; Large opening time context action link to troops fighting in Afghanistan

Photo by: Greg Downing. at   http://www.panoramas.dk/fullscreen2/full24.html
Petra, Jordan, sandstone cliff carvings, the Rose Red City, was the Treasury in the
'Raiders of the Lost Ark' starring Harrison Ford, also View architecture, inserted theme;
'I am strong, I have made a passage exalted into heaven.' Read from- 'Book of the
Dead' or, 'Coming Forth by Day' hieroglyphs hand reproduced by myself.

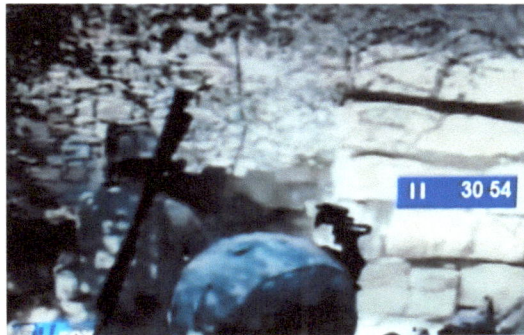

'Mammoth' View painting 2001; Blocks to match, Afghanistan 2009

can get away with or even think to attempt it, stems from their rampant Supremacy myth. Like Hitler, who thought he was descended from the Super Race of Atlanteans the inhabitants and supposed advanced society of the lost continent of Atlantis. Well, these new modern control freaks are like that. It is not at all Bleep or I. we are psi-normal, it is them now in power and it shows. Their word play shows all over the names they chose for things, and places to set up and spin off of. They try for bogus re-arrangements or downright lies actually. For instance they like to tell people I am a mental cripple a drunk and I used too much medical marijuana. In truth, I went for years without a puff of pot. I was going to the U of A attending Math and Physics and Philosophy classes. My marks were 7 to 8 out of 9. I did not toke or drink at all, nada. Nothing for years and years. I did Stained Glass after. You break the glass with your bare hands. You work with a soldering gun with the tip running 800 degrees. There is no time for shaking hands and hangovers. I painted immersed in Viewing for many years. I wrote I was creative. In short I have the work to show and the demeanour to prove I was not an alcoholic or any raging drug addict. Ever. And any time it did it was occasionally not as a problem. The problem is Nasa and the criminals that are insisting the Stargate is not viable when it clearly is. Finally, we wised up and gave them the undeniable boot. Now, to get them to accept it. Their egos are bruised and their agenda is to trash. So, we left. Literally, they are stalking us now. That will end when it is made public and they are forced to behave. I have the work to prove that stance. As for the Remote Viewing no one drunk or deranged could have achieved the results I did. Just not possible. They are merely covering, er, attempting to cover their own crimes against the Viewers. Again, see 'Remote Viewing: RAW' for more details on their, according to JAG the Navy Law terms, violation of my civil liberties. At this point bordering on kidnapping of a human.

With over two years of full time intense training by the Military's View trainer, as a Viewer working for the benefit of our side's Military, they are very wrong to attack us as in any way being charlatans or groupies. They are for whatever reasoning on their part, flat out wrong. These are not 'mental' they are valid Remote Viewing glimpses via Quantum Chromo Dynamics exploring the 5ᵗʰ. //Canada is not, I repeat not a freedom zone.

Some are seemingly determined to play Utopia now, during the Holy War and Anti Crusaderism ripe on our Continent. They seem to be into going, misinformed or not, ass up for Mo. If you are smart…well, the passport idea is still high on the list. I worry about the bad guys in the fall demanding Islamic bagging and gagging on our fair citizens. I worry, but we have our own men and security forces who are flexible, too. To counter and win over any onslaught on our peaceful communities the enemy and participants might have in mind for times to come.

If you see me leaving in the fall…you will know! They already gag censor from the White House for Islamic traditional silencing of opposition to their aims. All the missing folders and files and deleted parts in written documents, is gagging Islamic censorship. Not once under Pres. Bush did this happen. Our society simply doesn't practice censorship overruling our Freedom of Speech. We just don't. It is not only illegal it is not our way. If that happens I will be following the pint and the Ghost tip off to head for a great Walkabout in the land Down Under. Off to Australia as soon as and if they ever start Sharia enforcements. I would be worried here, they'll shut people in and block escape routes, since they are after Revenge and they won't want anyone to just flee their punishment.

//Three years ago, CNN did the Great Witch Hunt or what I called the Make Witch show. A real bona fide Inquisition on a Canadian. They are linked in actual sympathy for Tehran especially, and they detest our cameras, the British hunt Terrorists quite successfully, their MI5 is extremely competent at the hunt, and as a result the bad guys hate the cameras and of course by extension the Spies and Viewers in particular. They liked to hunt for years, to interfere with hunt of Islamic Terrorists. An occupational hazard to us in Viewing. Seems visual vanity is at the root of their obsession with the English folk lore and witches. The Iranian genetics has given their females a preponderance of large noses. Like the ones that show in our imagery in fairly tales and the like. It drives them to distraction such insult, intended or not. They are intolerant of them and over in their lands, they get them fixed with nose surgery when they can afford to. It suited them, their usual back at 'ya to the Security, to try to make me the witch 'doing' or 'spelling' instead. That's how an older Inquisition was arranged. Already done too. Closed files. So, they are doing some attempted remake, the Evil Genie theme. Wow, upgrading. A witch with a lamp. Their own silly twisted version of the lights on the trail. Their insistent, retaliation since I found this appropriate Bible verse the other day:

Philippians - New Testament   "Chapter One

1:27 Only conduct yourselves in a manner worthy of the gospel of Christ, so that whether I come and see you or remain absent I may hear Of you that you are standing firm in one spirit, with one mind striving together for the faith of the gospel.

1:28 in no way alarmed by your opponents which is a sign of destruction for them but of salvation for you, and that too from God.

1:29 For to you it has been granted for Christ's sake, not only to believe in him, but also to suffer for His sake.

1:30 experiencing the same conflict which you saw in me, and now hear *to be* in me.

Chapter Two

2:2 make my joy complete by being of the same mind maintaining the same love, united in spirit, intent on one purpose

2:3 do no thing from selfishness or empty conceit but with humility of mind let each of you regard one another as more important than himself.

2:4 do not *merely* look out for your own personal interests, but also for the interests of others.

2:5 Have this attitude in yourselves which was also in Christ Jesus.

2:6 Who although He existed in the form of God, did not regard equality with God a thing to be grasped.

2:7 but *emptied Himself taking the form of a bond servant and being made in the likeness of men.

*laid aside His privileges. "…

"2:15 that you may prove yourselves to be blameless and innocent children of God above reproach in the midst of a crooked and perverse generation among whom you appear as lights to the world."

Such timely sentiment, in this dark days, a few lights along the way.

//I use an ancient Egyptian View papyrus to hunt the Cultists who bring in only death, doom and gloom, couched in terms of tradition and duty.

VIEW painting of Aries from1970s with foreleg extended, match to running soldiers

Canadian soldiers in Afghanistan, and emote

herey-sesetoo   Master of
hry-sstoo   Secrets

VIEW water dinosaur outlined by white dots, a faint but regal glimpse of the head; tail

Counter Terror, we get to do things like say, 'Watch for an increase in child bombers blowing themselves up.' They are ramping up on the 7 to 10 year old. They want to cover for the Taliban paying for them, paying $4,000 to $17,000. For each child they buy to blow up. Counter. The life of the Spy in the Mailbox. Meanwhile these ever superior criminals and their ivory tower helpers, think security are too stupid and they need to see these abusers flaunting their 'win' to all of us. Not just police, they rankle pretty much all the spies and trip off the Military these days too, if your savvy and stuck watching. One lone example lately was when they wanted me to rent this cheapo shark movie to see and they would make links to it, to try to involve me before hand to one of their set ups. I tweeked to it and refused to watch the movie. The Law found 20 sharks filled with a ton of cocaine.

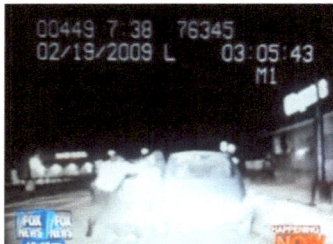

Cops in USA serving and protecting; FBI double checking; will the real UFOs....

View of a Dolphin; ship at bottom left; and a Policeman's cap; RV stick figure *emote*-Robot/Space Man from 'Day the Earth Stood Still' old version; RV security Bat

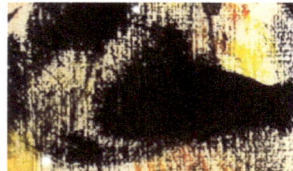

View swoop brush stroke 'Batman' figure in light, the Real Fire Fighters can get a good one going with their Spot lights; RV Fire Fighter's hat; RV emote of Seal; flippers

I would like to put to rest another spy legend on the not-so side of Storytime. A Viewer is not a 'Hancock' like in the Will Smith movie. And I watch all of his movies. Lots, big fan. But the powers that be, arranged for that. They did that movie after , years *after* this all here and they access and use accordingly, all the time. As they so wish, part of why they insist I am somehow their Genie. Well that movie and others, no really, use the Ripley's Believe it or Not condition comes with our modern and upgrade to Quantum now, society, well that script for Hancock was written deliberately to make it so. It was 'arranged' and still, we all know, that I don't 'do' things. That movie script was written 3 years after I was doing this. They already used us for 'Jumper' and others it was not new and it is not a real View script it was one of their 'paid' efforts. I don't include them at all. //I had to wake up today to these fools doing an Inquisition on me because I said my handlers had before made me wet myself. Now these politically motivated crashers, implying as if I was chasing the Seals. Pups that they are to an old doll like myself. No reflection on the Seals at all. Here is a neat View stick man of a Seal. View emotes are very empathically derived and visually descriptive. There is another one of Crocodile Dundee pointing and a matching emote or stick figure also pointing to show you better how these work, further along here. //
Just to be perfectly clear on that issue, I was not nor am I, chasing any Seal or any other man for that matter. A Stargate doesn't run itself. It's their own NASA head noise. Nothing to do with me, I helped with a VIEW of the Seals and their awesomely timed three simultaneous shots, when the Pirates were after a hostage event with a different ending. The wetting was some club thing or other I imagine. Like a form of joke, they do tests and other world shaking oddities to a Viewer, lots. You come to expect it, like the Spies and their constant coding. It was not because anyone at any time thought I was chasing any Seals. Hardly. I put them up on the site because they were great 3 at once shots and a good VIEW of it. The Pirate View theme involved linked directly in a future time frame to the Canadian Navy and their own chase of these Pirates. It is what we 'do' as Viewers. Tough if you have some pink jerks who don't like it. They beat on us, so, go find a dog to kick or whatever passes for fun to you. They told us on the news, they make the US Military Seals go to sleep wet. I

imagine it was some military training type stunt. To keep you in tune for when shit hit's the fan. They do that lots. I get tested plenty. The rest is your own sicko ideas being projected onto me and them. Telling them to knock it off has very little effect, sadly. Neither does blasting them, but I do on occasion, since I don't frankly care who they are! And sometimes it feels like who doesn't rag at me, rather than who is! Bleep agrees.

But you really need to get a serious hold of your own twisted nonsense being laid onto the humble Viewers. Although most Views are done using color here is the very first black and white View theme I painted, a descriptive visual View match to a US Navy under and above water Cormorant Craft.

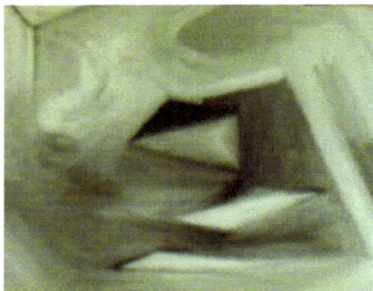

Stargate Remote View '06; US Navy Cormorant

The Israelis were and are forced to go into underground tunnels while they are attacked in their neighbourhoods their homes, to escape a nonsensical inconsistent attack by Islamic revenge squads. This is a basic comes with, in terms of any Islamic jihad hate task force setting up in or near or over the border from, any of our side's communities.

//In order to really attain a sustainable Utopia not just play shhh quiet for Jihad purposes, we need to wise up. When the Jihad is outlawed and the Muslims are integrated and busy being industrious not setting up to destroy. Then you can all go wow, it's Utopian workable.

Swell. Just saying. No no chasing. Admiring. Huge difference. Maybe you need to stop so much porn or whatever is rotting your brain. There are nice people out there. You meet some and you go , whew…just nice to know. There are still nice people out there. But snobs? They show. I am not overly impressed by wealth. Probably why I got this charming position. Oh sorry no complaining. Only these are enemy who were paid to torture! People listen to them, since they *work for Nasa* as though that phrase is some magical entitlement clause that bypasses all our laws and decency. What a gross predicament. No wonder this is surfacing so hard and fast the bends are not just in the road. The 'new guy' is Kingo of the world and too shy to tell his subjects. I am in my glory since the Governator the California Governor Arnold Schwarzenegger himself, recognized our Stargate. The cool View of the big knife he matched to the 'Commando' movie practice View and great knife. Adventure of course comes with its own brand of tribulations. I am often now punished for thinking creatively or making horrors a joke. Pakistan is doing it first. The Prime Minster of Pakistan As If Zardani is tracing the citizens' emails and texting and blog notes. If they find any jokes, shudder, about the Government they face 14 years in jail. I kid you not. I am experiencing this ridiculous restriction, too, more and more. Team O does not tolerate opposition. They are intent on control and censorship of our speech and actions as much as they can. No tolerance combined with merciless punishment. They are redoing the Nazis Henchmen. Replaying the 'Predator' and 'Terminator' action series of movies from our culture. …while we have 'Commando' and the 'Terminator'. And others. Huge relief. Since bad guys abound, this is a rather hostile Planet. Some of these bad guys (in abusing the RNM?) would love it if they could just steal a human's identity completely. A new zombie entity. Not happening to the Viewers, immune is immune. That zombie sending thing though, is what they are essentially doing when they 'take over' someone using RNM with out the victim knowing anything about it. Watching along here, doing Counter Terror while fiddling with the dials on the Time Tunnel, there are enough dots linking up to show a really serious misuse of a very serious weapon. I guess that depends on your point of view. To some of them, it is the perfect way to treat property of. What human rights. Sounds like Planet Ghoul and too many coloured brownies, but I assure you it is just a

Ca. Gov. Arnold Schwarzenegger brandishing the knife to match the View of it from his action movie 'Commando'

'Terminator' movie robot in California Governor Arnold Schwarzenegger's private office 2009; View match to this same artwork of the robot in 'Terminator'

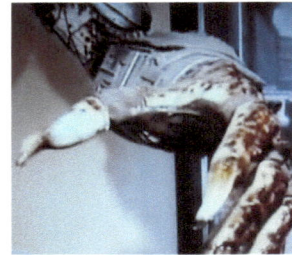

1. 'Predator'; 2. psi Remote Viewed painting, Predator's claw (3D); 3. close up of

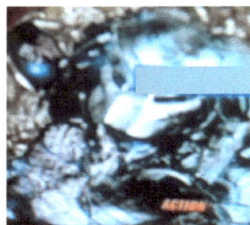

A) 'Predator' starring Ca. Governor A. Schwarzenegger, movie visual of Predator's front face plates. B) Match to troop's back just barely showing as he walks out of the frame, in the corner at bottom right in the photo.

modern Top Secret program now coming into the light of day, so far as Stargate and Remote Viewing are concerned. Abused RNM is another thing entirely. The targeted person is unaware of the 'hidden suggestive' and 'suasion'. The normally harmless psi link is being unleashed on our gentle Christian flocks. Bad guys are in setting up blinds for arrangements for their side to take over and enforce their ways over ours. Will they succeed? Likely not, but that doesn't mean they are not in and trying or going to make us suffer and even fight them to get our usual Freedom back from them! Our freedom has been on their chopping block since 1865 when they freed the Slaves, according to how some of them are carrying on. They aired the Reverend Jeremiah Wright. They are so used to tuning it out they didn't even comment on it. It was most unusual for a reply to the Rev. Jeremiah Wright and his "chicken's *coup"* reference. They think we are all chickens and sheep belonging to the Lord Christ's flock. They are so alarmed they had their bad guys over in Swat, Pakistan going through the motions of literally picking up guns, meant as spy chat. As in 'quick they're arming themselves'. They prefer us unarmed, it would only spoil their planning and interests. And now in the States, they have North Com threatening Fema Camps for....who exactly? What is it, intrigue terror now? Ancient cloned Mammoths, by some over indulgent rich Clubber, rampaging loose over our continent. Just another version of King Kong. It is insidious and the native Far Easterners who are integrated and happy to be over here in no, really, Safe land, are likely crawling out of their skins watching this Hamas in Hoods setting up, and a black wave is pulling over our lands ....they call is 'Creeping Sharia' I call it creepy Sharia. They have a fit if you are not behaving according to them, and they really only allow forced labour and moral restrictions a stone would have trouble with over here in freedom land. Jihadists are in attacking Christian Americans. Some of them are in denial, and it is a hurtin' show watching it progress. Basically they are the flocks unprotected by their own under this current status quo. Atrocity in the making. It's their America and their Freedom and Culture. They're American. I would not want to be the one attacking them. Islam gave Osama a Sword when the Queen of England gave Salman Rushdie a Knighthood. He wrote the 'Satanic Verses'. They're still blowing fuses over it. /I am seriously getting my passport to

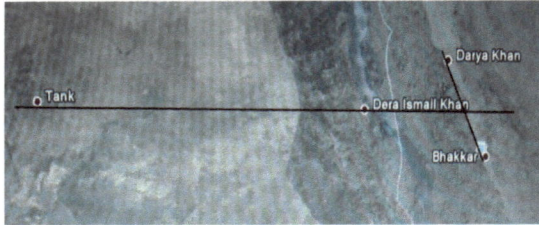

Bin's Sword of Gideon seen as a Viewer Google tourist. Runs through Tank at the tip, and has Dera Ismail Kahn next on the horizontal; Darya Khan- Bhakkar crossing;

bail to Australia. Nothing for rescue so far. In the fall you will see some real sheep with bark then. Good thing we do have Military protection. Exposed and all as the Goat feels these days, watching them tweak '1984' down below us and oozing over our border. They, meaning our Military might, are not nailed down. These bad guys are now showing signs they are getting all upset hearing the Christians are in fact arming. Sheep with big fangs. Mutant sheep. That the enemy forces access and get their own copy of this Spy Eye tool, is already a given to us on our side over here, since back prior to the US election start up campaigns last year, just when they had Ahmadinejad run those wee motor boats at the large US Navy ships. For whatever slick reasoning. O Team is just making sure they are all comfy. But they are attempting to use this script to step up to the American and Canadian Navy, as well. I don't think they are past the Navy yet. This is certainly not their anything, not even our own side's Nasa can attest to control. Stargate belongs to the Future of humanity on its way to the Star Trails. No Space Pirates are going to interfere, that's Fate. It is written. This is really bothering them. More than these good flocks of happy Christians are being alerted to. Some are though, aware we likely are in for some nasty surprises from another culture even now quietly sneaking up on us, like they are the cat stalking us, the prey. They're it online anyway. I don't make plans, I write books, and do remote viewing and paint. Very da Vinci and Code. The rest of the Spy work is up to just the steady leak thing, informed and informing, like a drip here and there. See what happens in the future. It is not my main priority. But it gives me good RV focus. Yeah they're serious or they would not be so censoring. And they really are abusing rnm and it really does have to be handled sooner or later. It's not going away until you realize it and someone does something or the shit hit's the fan. Looks like its' the old 'wait until the shit hit's the fan ' solution. Might go down fast after that. When it is undeniable if they don't act, others will move them aside as it has happened before right here on Earth. Details differ, but it happens. The top goes bad, not all…but some or most or..lots or…here it is victims of RNM and the Forces, but it is still real. And they are not 'their usual'. /The Americans are inside invading personal computers and deleting and inserting and all manner of utterly contemptible and thoroughly disgraceful hacking and criminal intent being actualized. Big Brother is inside snipping away and it is already showing. No, I can't sound any alarm. Stargate provides an Oracle and we can do what I am doing warning and …looking ahead. Others do the 'doing' as per usual. I just ramble on. Not rambo on. No one needs to trash this that is for sure. The sceptics make it sound like I just swirl shit around. They are like someone looking at one of the 3D graphics and saying it doesn't work., just because they don't know how to hold it to their nose and pull it away! Others who do know how are amazed they are carrying on like they are and not learning how to understand the Views of Stargate. It's not that hard. They're just too snobby to put anything up to their noses! The rest of the people will laugh at them when they learn this truth. No one is burying Hypershift and 'gee anyone who goes to mars would have to stay there' is so lame Nasa you need to give back your pay. I was there and back in under 4 minutes, now, that's what you aim for, Teleports. Star Trail Hypershift, like that…you go! You don't just do the Nasa revolving dinning room around the solar system for eternity and call is the Space program. Use STARGATE. Gee, …Just skip them, they are not worth it and they are certainly not with it. Hitch to the Stars …that's how I did it. And Bleep brought us Stargate. I have done this for over 3 years, and they keep ragging at me tonight about too much medical marijuana. I barely toke at all. And further more in our society as a free citizen I am entitled to go out and get good and stinking drunk if I so wish, Especially important to get that straight with them doing the commie Big B traced on your computers never mind just online, they brought in special ops help on that one. For an RV paint done in under 4 using psi link hot modern chi

US Marines in fierce fire fight Afghanistan 2009; RV they both raised their guns in one swift simultaneous movement; chopper in Afghanistan

Remote View psi-chi paintings of Marines in Afghanistan; match to elements in photos

View of dark end of Choppers in photo at left, Afghanistan, 2009; RV emote- 'synch'

it is awesome in its precision and capsules of descriptive info. Positive advancement with certain achievable results involving the Necker type Hyper shift. Typical Earth, some of them are blocking RV not being able to see and recognize anything but artistic realism as something valuable. It's their personal preference, and it's creating obstacles where there should be only development and research. Clean and unhampered. They fail to understand. No comprehension of creative works, as such let alone this cutting edge inter-dimensionality, unfortunately. I figure these guys are not getting past Earth, as they are, anyway. I imagine the Galaxy likely would destroy our planet if they took over and achieved the ability to get into outer space with anything as sinister as Inter-Galactic offence. We need to get them removed anyway, it is just more reason to. They're not going anywhere. There is no Jihad allowed on Mars. That's an entirely understandable and necessary to include in your considerations of our real time Earth abilities and events as they occur, an Inter-Galactic condition. Definitely linking to a greater cosmic 'us' like that exemplified in 'Star Wars' starring Harrison Ford another stellar Viewer. Just not as fancy. I guess I should go to the mall and see if I can get a copy. I liked it anyway. Probably expensive his shit is. Was. That was Total Recall and oh, Predator terms. Yeah, no they're going to just blow the planet before they let these guys unleash on the Galaxy. With timelight shift that fast and you think what, no one else has it? Right. Grow up. The No Jihad is a non-negotiable strictly enforced condition. We Earthlings really do need to get that straight. The media damn well need the lesson so they will start telling it right such as the JIHAD is not over and it desperately needs to be banned. Sharia, head scarves, face gear, the works. Gotta go. Zero tolerance. Round up that behaviour and stop it as surly as those Japanese internment camps. This is War and it is our lands. Our people's freedom to protect. There is no alternative, no compromise. They banned Sharia in the Province of Ontario that looms on the map over the Great Lakes in Canada. With the bulk of our cities and most of the population.
And that's what is coming in so it has to be handled, or it won't be pretty the mess it makes as we all Revolt. No matter how capable you all are. They're in like Alien, they're infested with Jihad's creeping Sharia in North America. It's IN, they can't fight …but they will. We all will. We

will fight for our Freedom. And the more they take the more certain and swift that will be. It seems to be in long time planning and highly organized. And with horrific weapons at their disposal and no souls all revenge. It's aim and intent. They're a ….wow. Anyway it is the youth who have the Future ahead of them. A Free Future is our one and only aim. Not a quiet submission, a peaceful Freedom. As per usual, and we all know full well what it is we prefer.

/Ray Bradbury did Mars too. Only , in his books they did what Nasa just suggested for their idea of modern Space Exploration. They went and didn't just come back. These guys are doing it like it is pre-computer days, never mind pre-Quantum Leap. They're so out of date it is pathetic. Additionally, they lie. And they all know it, or soon will when they learn these entitled snobs didn't release to them the astounding results of the Phoenix Lander Race. I set a new speed record. I surpassed the speed of light using psi, proved it beyond doubt and they will not acknowledge that they already know this to be a fact. I had back up Art Views on the patch of ice underneath the Lander they found on Mars, too. It's a priceless discovery they are trashing Space Exploration itself! Attempting to. They need to be removed. They will be in time, that's another certain prediction. Some things just are. Miracles and everything….hoping they're always hoping. Depends on what end of the stick you're on. I did see a beaver in one it was yesterday? I think. He sure looks like he is pointing. Paul Hogan in 'Crocodile Dundee' script and actor; linked View (next page). Yeah I seem to have picked up a Ghost. They do that. /each one of these paints could be a different star map for all I bleeping know. But I have to tell you I had _____ down as Crocodile Dundee until I saw Paul Hogan wrote the script. Now, that's a View Point. See. Very highly descriptive. A Future Stargate has materialized. We can sense it. Realize there are Stargates and one is Open- Past, Now, Future…

Very 'Terminator' movie too, since he came back in time for saving humanity too. See the Archer being described visually? That is the center of the Milky Way our own Spiral Galaxy, towards Sagittarius A. So, the center, wow. Hey, Team O and your International Organization, get ready to meet the Intergalactic Center Crew. Mathematically it works out to faster than the speed of light. All the math I need to know. The distance to Mars and the speed of Light. Houston you got company. And they do the z like no sheeft. Z= red shift and blue shift. ZED in MIB. The USA Chiefs have in their possession an intergalactic RNM ability we must insist is *always and only, wielded responsibly*. Who would think this is a dead Universe? Why would you think that ? ....at low velocities z=v/c and using the relativistic shit, they have one example where v/c= blah blah blah=0.92 about a quasar receding with a velocity 92% the speed of light. Red shift that is 'z' here, is an objecting receding. Blue shift, appears to us when an object is approaching. This is in time context significant too, since we are indeed attempting to surface a program formerly with the same secrecy as the real Stealth craft. Viewing is not a new discipline. Used as an Oracle with a back up to security and tips function. We do search just like others who seek to attempt rescue. A busy challenging skill set, with a marked psi component to being a Viewer. The craft, as described, in these Viewing visuals, are understood as *approaching in this instance* because of their color pink then blue, at a typical outcome position lower. VIEW Space/Stealth-ish visual of ship - computer negative enhanced, z=red shifted ship, z=blue shifted; approaching. As well as the visual to match from the movie 'Stealth'; Views being descriptive as well.

Approaching Alien craft in the descriptive and tailing as a light show, for pattern recognition in that end portion of a Shuttle taking off for the ISS (International Space Station). The light pattern looking like a great match. So, taking this arrangement into consideration to read the message, that the View is here and now describing to us. In fact under these time's specific circumstances of extreme new and frightening consequence it can also be seen as a warning to spur us to an adequate response. Perhaps you have unleashed and are letting them continue to unleash an horrific mind control invasion weapon to commit torture on other human beings in itself horrendous. And in particular in the case of the Viewers, for example, psi talents with many years Viewing in Deepside and many connections of an inter-Galactic nature. Among other things, a totally unconscionable event. I just hope you are ready for the horror these creepsters are potentially, but not necessarily unrealistically, drawing to this Planet. If they are on their way. Keep up with your mind twister, torture and invasion of humans toys and see what potentially,

Canadian soldier in Afghanistan pointing, over a white helmet; View emote stick figure; Paul Hogan creator of 'Crocodile Dundee pointing; Special Ops; USS NY Christening

Canadian troops Afghanistan 2009

original oil 2006

Shuttle lift off, image 'ship'; Blue shift; Computer negative red shift ship

Deepside and Deeper Aliens with shall we say, ethical considerations, and Vacuum Zones to protect (recall 'Total Recall' starring the Governator, Arnold Schwarzenegger). What would they be permitted to do to you as a result? And on that note, take the stone agers and blocks down with you. Make sure you keep using RNM abusively, and it is going to look good on you when your cosmic arrogance and denial backfires on you. And that's if they 're poking along…or do you think they are out there going, hey big O, how's it hanging bro. gonna aim that cool ray over on our way? The _____ is hacking others not just me. They will censor any work that reveals their ulterior agenda. The other pill, in other words. Bet they got 'law'. we may not need Aliens. But they sure don't need mind farms! Bet they got the independence too. Cause damn That's being realized. Nasa was the base. They would likely come in if they think machines or soul less ghouls abusing mind control weapons on humans irresponsibly and murderously. No, Viewing is not the problem but RNM abuse most certainly is. We may be heading for a planetary extinction! Panthers, South African horrors and…The list is too long and unspeakable. I think the bad guys think they will show you instead. Here, I found my Bin's manifesto. The one they all seem to be following along to. As they do their obligation to their beliefs. The commoner's solution. If you want it you go buy it. Done. The fat cats at the top can shove their memos right up there with their self righteous attitudes. Like they did with our Rights. Yeah those real American trucks in Real America are not the shiny brand spanking new painted ones, the huge painted ones they are sending and using up here. No comparison. They paint them for we are the success, O Team show up here in Canada. I censored the evil jerks in the whitey now dark arts house. I used tv dial on off. Gosh the invaders here are not dressing like the ones they had at the gun ranges in America. Not openly …yet. Just alluding to it. /I was thinking the hieroglyph for Range the two markers and the walking legs out of their a to b descriptive might be that Australia is out of range of their vicious assault weapon. The media. If I need to and if these fools start bagging and gagging for their religious 'rights' and slaughtering Christ I will move there to get my normal heterosexual female human rights back. Sorry CIA Chief, Leon

Panetta, you're not invited. Go 'do' the goat. He gets lonely. So who is XXXX? Good one. No it is not too much medical marijuana. One of their favourites to use to harass and slander me. You are censoring, removing my folders off my PC. Never mind I found it. They do remove them these days. No really. That 'What? Not more death threats! They took the entire folder. Good thing I had just made more copies of it recently. They're too much. /these guys are at it again. Hawk, they're nasty. Integrate? No wonder they were told not to integrate. We won't be putting up with it. . Their invasion is over before it began. There is no way in hell we will let them take over and shut down our essential as air to breath Freedom. Not at all. And now that they think they will control us, There could conceivably be a battle yet to come, reminiscent of those famous ancient Oracle words …*wooden walls.* Chernobyl translates as wormwood. These are dots and they're adding up…View Prophecy. Call it whatever you like. It's the 5ᵗʰ and it is very very real. As real as the Future, it is not yet fully realized as other than raw potential, but that doesn't mean it is not Real. These are certainties. The Uncertainty Principle on one end the Certainties on the other. In a SpaceTimeLight structured Universe the Future is a Certain as the Past. It is the present that is elusive. That's why the value on Zen. And I seem to have lost my H folder, the hieroglyphs I would not put it past them to trash it, they are obsessed and horrified I use them to hunt their Al Qaeda and all. / That Will Smith movie the 'Wild Wild West' oddly enough had those neck blow up things on them and they had to 'stay within range' you must be able to get out of range…seems to be a possible that it is referring to, to get out of range. The Panetta lion strength symbolism. The stars are another range. The Sphinx pointing to Leo in the sky connection. I will work on it. If there is a range here, on Earth in terms of strength of their waves then why would it also be able to go so far into space and why would there be a range ON the earth AND a different range (space distance being so large) out in space? Why would it be limited here at all if it goes so far into space? Goodness, letting them do ruin and trash our system, and security. Since you're letting him it is your own fault then, to some degree. Me, I don't get any choice under the new he has rule of the world trip. Leaving is not an option. No matter how much I tell them they would be better off without having me falsely imprisoned. However it is not just me, bet there are more who are truly outraged than their arranged 'polls' show… crocodile/no they keep trying to make me watch their jacko ghoul so they can assault my sensitivities and I guess they get to lie in the states and say I am into, hold onto your sensibilities now, dead ghoul perverts! I have no idea and I really don't care what they think down in any cess pool, where ever it may be. I feel sorry for anyone down there who is stuck there under horror that the media entitlement to slant organizing, brought in on them. They seem to be just barely getting the idea out now that it is a total disaster so far as our Western civilization is concerned. Barely. They're still sticking up for it way too much if you ask me. Bet I am not alone on that one. And yes, they are hideous and ghouls and yada yada. Now I know what it meant when they said in Raiders as the bad guys tried to open the ARK, 'don't look' …all they are doing is trashing me today. I have the tv off. They keep saying Sometimes I think that they all just want to drive all opposition insane. Really is that all of them? Or just their own RNM and paid jerks? Or do they have a US Poll number on it….wouldn't be the Jihad at the Universities would it? Or the mad anti Crusaders out to destroy our establishment and fail in terms of our honour and progress. They just had my heart racing again until I thought JAG and they stopped. I was in getting the wet towel ready….Just for the record I earn everything I do around here. I was just done with the heart racing thing, start up, then I made breakfast to let it get cold while I fussed with the download I didn't want anyway, and had to get the blocks off it that I didn't even know, up at 3:30 am but I refused to get up until 5:30 it is too hard on me the half sleep time and Tehran and AL Qaeda for punishment. The bad guys want them to keep me under Torture status. Inquisition at best. And that entails sleep deprivation. So they slave the Viewers continuously and now, under hassle and torture at their whims. And they whim a lot. Well, they get bugging me endlessly. A revamped entirely ruthless, silly Inquisition. /I think some of the sceptics are upset that I painted a claw in 3D paint technique during my last View painting session. All under the 4 minutes for timing, as per usual. And I try to explain to them that , no, it is not spooky that is how paint works too. Lots of artists paint with large globs of paint. You really need to go visit a big art institute size art gallery. You are way off base to think that painting and Viewing are 'make scary'. Get a grip. And acrylic paint, the really modern shit is really good for 3D affects you can build. You just are not aware of the quality and versatility awarded to the creative and Art in our culture. All there is that we involve in paint, or creativity or the 5ᵗʰ D or viewing. You really don't. I am not kidding about the Art Gallery …go visit a Gallery that carries more than just Realism artists, go to a creative Art Gallery. A large one like the Louvre or the Chicago Art Institute Boston for example, have them too. The really big old ones with plenty of Master's selections and kinds. Then come and say 'wow really spooky'. Paint is 3d build-able and that's just reality. //NASA is criminally stalking Stargate. Attempting to disguise it as just regular activity. It is way over the line. At this stage they are past being evil paparazzi. I already said I am very forgiving *if they stopped,* but they refuse to stop and they're at this point stalking. Anyway, Bleep and I are ousting them from our Stargate endeavour. And that's final. This Star Trail is OPEN. //Working more counter terror as per usual, as this account this running daily Viewing Report unfolds. Seems in the Fox cable script we follow, they are using it now to substitute and reinforce their info gleanings and messaging, spy chat, using search and google…avoiding web bots or whatever they call them, the spiders that look for things. They are calling them the New Black Panthers now. A very transparent agenda showing in such a slight but search significant change. Designed to throw any trackers of their actions off their trail. Covering their tracks. //Those painted trucks they send up to Canada, er, likely paint in Canada, since that's showing like fresh paint, no on the road usage marks, as you would normally see on vehicles with mileage; you can tell. Those trucks are like having a fence and only painting the neighbours side. Like a Syrian nuclear phoney front on it. They do Hollywood Movie Stunts and Sets. All for the Show. Al Qaeda loves the Show. So does Tehran. …and that is who was banned from the mall, the guy whose things were censored, and he had to leave an American mall, it was anything Al Qaeda or Iranian jokes. They are not tolerating jokes. And that's what is now operating with impunity out of America! Man, does it ever show when you know. Continuing to grow and spread out. Like that chokeweed in a garden until it is so bad things

are being choked out and anyone even glancing at it will see a disaster not a garden. Our people will handle it as inevitably as Fate. Like referred to in the Bible, Chapter of Jobs, I must watch the movie 'Mission Impossible' again, get that photo I dropped. They are censoring and we are ratting like crazy since the West is not going to like running into any color House sponsored censorship. They keep hearing it and seeing it, they're going to start a rumble they won't be able to ignore. //Oh I get it, that one Black Panther at the voting station last vote in the USA was a look alike. They are using them on me all the time steady a matter of routine it is in their normal M. O. they were doing Che's lower South representation so the Spanish and Africans pushing North to invade know they are welcome. They have the guns and the new legal, for backing. They are the strong arms out front, on the other side, not friendly to our side. Black Socialism, sort of. More, really. //Humouring the Inquisition. Not that I am an alcoholic since I am not, but I will take another updated photo of that same bottle. For proof just for you. If I was a drinker with a problem it would not still be here, I assure you. Especially with the mess going on lately. In response to the local moveon.org's demands on me, I would like nothing better than to move on, however I am busy being falsely imprisoned, Civil Rights violations aside, tortured, stalked and they also attempt murder on me according to their own program. So, got any other ideas? The Zeds for the blue shift red shift, two z modes, two z descriptives are likely the Mr. Aziz they just let out of 'house arrest' in Pakistan in April this year, in other words a couple of months ago. He doesn't want Muslim males killed. He still believes in legal Jihad in Pakistan and wherever else they insert into. Jihad, the legal according to them, non tolerance and killing of other than their own ways. That would also include the expendable kids/women/ and now Al Q using horses, it is the Muslim men he was set free to aid with. Their Prime agenda.
Mr. Aziz was held in ahem, house arrest, after the Red Mosque attack. He was escaping dressed in a large dark flowing full robe the females must wear, for Islamic dress codes and moral imperatives the Burka. They are on about some guy cross dressing in the US news right now. That's likely coded for Mr. Aziz since I typed in the zed shift. Their 'friendlies'. He was a big supporter of suicide bombings the news script says. Thousands

attended his they called it a sermon …he said they are a peaceful people, however if their aim is blocked (bin does the True Way and Iran Ahmadinejad at the University did the True Way) then there is a witness factor, and that's courts talk and about like the earlier in Iraq Blackwater fiasco where they had instant and continuous witnesses galore after the fact. So many it was, well, arranged. According to them, witnesses to the scenes in Swat and in Fata as it says in the article, Swat Valley and Federally Administered Tribal Areas. With the Red Mosque and an adjacent school compound. So this is the same old ramped their attention has been on getting their Safe Haven back ever since the Red Mosque. In Pakistan under this current Holy War Aziz is a huge deal to them. Represents fighting for their Shari and it's peculiar moral behaviour codes still operating in our day and age. We do digital as a culture and they still do Sharia and it's enforcement wing, Jihad using Mujahideen, the Islamic Holy Warrior. Like their Lion Shayk Osama bin Laden. Mosques, schools, red, sermon, supplies, burkas, kids and women and anything other than muslim men as bombs…this is Aziz and Zardari the one who gives out 14 years for any joke about him and investigators and tracing the people email, blogs and texts…censorship …make that Sharia and censorship. The censorship is here now, I can attest to that one. It is not any part of my being held to do this service=Slavery since it wasn't like that at all under Pres. Bush the American non Islamic President. So the Sharia is the *Silent Talk* here. The Red Mosque battle by Pakistani Army under Musharraf was fought when the guys decided to try to take advantage of the West fussing for the women's rights. Arabia didn't like it either. It is a put down to their customs and Sharia Courts, for the Koran. So they got their new secret- You can't shoot they are women!- forces out into the community from the Red Mosque (shades of Acorn) and they were happy trashing cds, radios, dvds, lipstick anything modern. It was a Jihad = behaviour Koran dictates enforcement squads…like our cops for our laws. Only they were using the full cover look burka gang, this was just before the Gang took the Vote in Pakistan. Full cover, they were not even showing their eyes openings in some. Full and they were using men in under this full cover. Witness - Aziz fleeing in a Burka during the Red Mosque incident where the bad guys were trying to enforce Sharia standards on locals as victims. The Pakistani Army got them. Recently however, the Pakistani President Zardari released him. Actually it was over two months ago. That's the none spoken chat today. It is safe haven community, jihad,….designed to protect only the Muslim men. The Afghanis get a bit jealous seeing it and they want safer havens and good nights rest for their men too. It mentions siege too. As a 'potent symbol'…that's another community based 'stability' measure. Oh that's right congress put money in their budget for 'community stabilization' using acorn now renamed. The double entendre is the stable the harem the horses, Al Qaeda and Arabia. Notably Iraq has horses, in fact they ran their horse races all through the War in Iraq even during the worst days. They showed theirs prior to the Arabian show prior to the Derby. One of the news channels did 'chat trash English script' after the infidels won the Derby. They acknowledged the Canadian connection. One of the trainers of the winning horse was Canadian. They linked it to the torture exhibit they put on for us pre race. They did the naming of the horses that Arabia entered in the Derby to go with the King's family video clip of how Arabia torture's in the desert. They like the 'how to' as attempt to explain their rational to us heathens, of the uncovered and flamboyant kind. A wee torture event, that the media showed parts of just before the Derby. Exposing a desert torture theme. The caterpillar Torture method was all the rage in the new Administration's talk attacking the former administration's CIA for using it on their own as distinct from our own …they started the real vicious torture on Bleep and I, immediately. But that's all in the book 'Remote Viewing: RAW' and we at Stargate are aiming beyond that hysterical nonsensical behaviour on the part of the powers that be. What I wrote 'RAW' under, was raw Torture, and that's just how it was. Sometimes, still having its moments when it ought not to be. // Aziz is on my mind to day. Not 'moving along now'. Sorry, you would understand if they were inside you torturing for their own ways over ours, too, I would imagine. Funny how that works. His name was Maulana Abdul Aziz. The chief cleric of the Red Mosque. The Maulana is the Black Panthers a radicalized group of Africans in America. As a Terrorist theme, they do *mauling*, like the Bengal tigers the zoos and the release of large cats, they do the malls they bomb night clubs like at Bali.

That tower, Bala Hissar Citadel. I named a 2ⁿᵈ paint post 9/11 of the towers with symbolism Citadel. It stands for the stronghold at the front of a city. //I agree. Declare Victory and come home, but for different reasons, they just want you all out of their lands so they can be Muslims in Muslim lands with no tolerance of outsiders showing or building. I think we need them. Coming up. If they don't get their Sharia I am afraid it will almost be worse than if they did! Not really both are about as bad, take your pick. We could see a series of attacks either way. The focus shifting to the Sword…if they don't get their way. And they really really won't and they really are here. They blended in much better today. I was grateful. I was fussing about some other lame thing and I was glad to, it kept my focus and attention off them for a change I am sick of them interfering with a normal walk. But I am very aware they were there and watching and acting just far more subdued, told to appear normal, carry on as

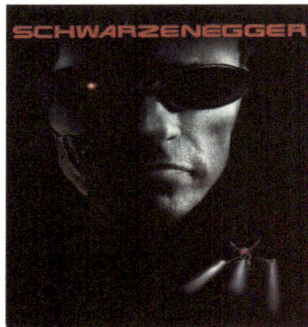

sedoo: traveller

Citadel View 2004; California Governor Arnold Schwarzenegger 'Terminator' poster; RV emote of the Red eye; vehicle with similar red light, Iraq, 2009

unobtrusively as they could I saw them all doing it I took few photos. A few of one buildings cars, arranged, and then none. I wrote down no plates. They merged in. they were still there. We won't know them all for 'proved and certain' anyway but the hunted can tell when they are still being stalked. They were still there. And that's intent. They are here for a reason. They are the recon force. They are in and acclimatizing. They are getting more familiar on their routes and not so obvious. They now know I am 'normal ' appearing and it is not such a big deal . One gawked the others, well maybe a few looked…they were far more blended in. there is more words on the side of the article I am reading about Aziz it mentions 'whitestone journal: fighting real parrots with a fake owl'…an unusual enough article. I will scan it in for you./learning guns, they are interesting. Hard to keep my mind on it. That's a big book when I do this too. I will do the best I can. No promises.

//mauling: tiger tiger night club car filled with gas cans, nails shit like that a nasty mix. UK out side the club a blue Mercedes I think it was…or a silver and a green I would have to look it up…there were two one down a bit …both rigged to blow smoke and smell gave them away when they were going to be towed for parking violations. That's pretty bleeping 'luck' if you want to know. …tiger woods, perhaps. Sports. They release large cats in the states, literally, they go into the zoos and bleep with them. Let them out deliberately. Their jungle India-Paki familiars the large cats. They have cheetahs in Iran, too up in the salt flats. Why a cat would want to live there I have no idea. They used them in the desert scene in Hidalgo too. That Horse Race was up along the side in IRAQ. They're …doing (another dong; that's taepo dong, the North Korean threats, we watch for typos that signal a psi pick up on links to security risks; watching them) names …these days. Usually for a norm. Something to watch. So I said blue shift and friends and they did the …friendly and thoughtful conversation. Just mentioning how I read them. But you don't want it you want me to 'move on' …sorry, just the counter terror habit. Sounds like maybe NY. Note: the very next day after typing that in, they released a big cat from an Illusion magic show in Las Vegas in the States. Not too subtle. More like flaunting lately. //I will rag on the Queen of England if I think they are off on the wrong track. I don't play any favourites, other than the Mars Knights, of course. The British Monarchy is usually clean. Sometimes they get advised and I have a fit over something they do or not. Sometimes I am wrong. Sometimes they are wrong. It is WAR we don't get A.S.S. memos. I don't anyway. The photo in this story a couple of months ago was about the red mosque and they showed a 'bullet riddled ' car…you mentioned riddled in the talk. Something about riddled it reminded me of the joker theme. Something. They did not have a lot of cars to be riddled with bullets at the Red Mosque. It is not a main event photo of that battle. It is an odd specific. Bullet riddled cars. You do the math. I know it was our side mentioned it. So, tweaked? Intuition? Something? I am just mentioning the obvious connection. Back to learning gun. They are on about the kinds of beer like wine cellars and fine bouquets. It's a beer. Drinking beer (image) but still upper establishment in demeanour. It is a financial division. A put down to the commoner.//Just done the deal in Swat for Islamic Law …in the 'restive north western region of swat' they *usually* say the 'formerly restive' it is a notable omission. Or, an indication of happy Sharia campers? Their hacker tale that I type in mentions 'former cia and former sen.' …the last line of the article is 'It is a virus for which there is no cure in the foreseeable future' talking about aziz and the red mosque and intolerance and violence. Not up to me, not my jihad, not my invasion. Back to learning gun. At the very bottom in 'related searches' it has Pakistan get email alerts Ghazi, Maulana Abdul Aziz. I think Abdul is the name of the al masri isn't it? Hang on…no he is AYYUB Abu Ayyub al Masri the other pink marked bad guy. He was in Baghdad, hails from Egypt. Might be up in the fight. Says he is also known as ABU HAMZA AL -MUHAJER. And that's the holy Mujahideen they use up there….he is the one who always instructs them to each kill one american…to help out. Do their part. Initiate individual attacks. 'urging muslims to join the fight' could be in on the online recruiting too. In the schools they are right now. Viruses. And computer infections. Schools and china and censorship gone mad out of the WH. The malls booting as in commie censoring, any talk that is anti AL Q and Iran. Wow, the very two we know beyond doubt they let use this, accessing our side's security works. Irresponsible doesn't begin to cover it. It's RNM at the bottom of this atrocity. Sorry guys there is no moving along not yet. They're still here setting up to do their thing their thing is not peace it is the opposite they think peace is us gone and quiet. Quiet = censorship. Freedom gone. Controls in. Community and school *district*, based, that being their chat term in the script on the tv, today. The bad guys are now in using the teens, means the high schools are up for conflict and anarchist issues. Not just the Universities (insertions)…more talk of car bombs. In the Abu Hamza al Masri article. Financially, bombing the cars. As well as the other norm. If they could do it and not have it stand out so we would all know undisputedly it was Terrorists bombing here and bring the heat down on them, they would. //More troubles from the States. Again, I am tuning into events while I write here, too. Seems too 'convenient' they pulled that stunt in Hollywood, Florida. RNM signature, name word play. There are real political and religiously opposed to Christians, who are intent on destroying our entire Society and Security in every way they can manage and then some. Translates into, it's our *Freedom* they are attacking! Using the intel agencies in America. Like a modern goon squad. Attempting to smash STARGATE, both of us, and the Police and Military. RNM abuse under Team O and Acorn. Using the media as Medusa. They have EMP capabilities, if they are still operative. The book 'Raw' explains what's up.

Or Shoot the Machines, Clubs. No one is going to object when they hear what was being done, used and abused and the aim and intent and how extensively used, it was becoming clear to see. Causing mass murders and now lately swarming as their tactics of choise. They did a swarm on me going outside tonight, as punishment for typing in comments on an article about how Al Qaeda is using the small children wrongly. It no doubt offended them. So, the solution? Sledgehammers. Or, the 'just shoot them' suggestion. Sounds about right. Turn your fire sprinklers on. I guess that's dangerous…stand back…then shoot them…or, emp emp emp emp …or I don't know shit. However your SWAT does….I typed in Leon and that range with the lion for strength hieroglyph visual. They object to my using Egyptian visuals so they punish me. They use the RNM wave capability they have these digital modern days, ramped on me. As well as a real live force of invaders, would be the most accurate description. Currently there is a growing knowledge that these bad guys over here, are officially organizing, in order to take us all out, one way and another. All pointing to the links in a slave class chain they're building. As surely as the sun rose yesterday. Learning schedules, habituating themselves into our communities. Blending in like an invading Alien force. NSA monitoring team? or some training devise from hell. Hard to say once you're down that rabbit hole in the Quantum tunnel, spy chat replacing emails.

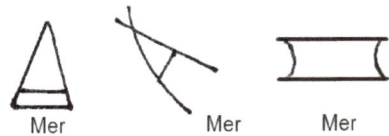

Mer   Mer   Mer

'Grey Day' horse (Winnipeg, Canada field; photo by *Journal*) NATO Secretary General is Anders *Fogh* Rasmussen; note how horse's legs match Egyptian Hieroglyphs for Mer; timely links to the front shape on the soldiers' guns

caution always. //Meanwhile, back here in Canada. Easy, could be these invasion forces are intending to swarm us, as a reflection of their hive mentality. When it was used under bush it was to keep us working us, not just apply methods to get the War handled, using Viewers and handling it as such. The aim was entirely different. Take that and combine it with their current media focus and paraphernalia all running on a distinct visual course of white pale heads/faces and dark round ghoul's eye. Inner African continent asserting control over the white folk. Using powerful magic and spirits. Hey, don't look at me, I am just reporting the current visual trends overruling in America right now. A concurrent with if you like, to the other line of dictation, a rearrangement of all according to each of them following his scripted performance. So knowing the great folly of our entertainment fed society and the insidiousness of the Sharia and the hideousness of the bad guys now in charge and attacking innocent humans at their pleasure, using RNM. I have instructions on how to block them if they start ramping it on the masses. Really they need to be shut down. But, there are some timely and perhaps who knows, necessary even, to the Future of humanity on Earth and the ability of a revolutionary minded citizenry to

withstand such an horrific onslaught. Instructions on how to deter and interfere with the thought wave psi *emf* wavelengths (JAG the Navy lawyers had to take the NSA in the USA to trial over abuse already, before. Not my imagination, unfortunately.) combined with a modern day digital ramp, The abused RNM they are using and perfecting as they charge along on a Conquest mission. That all said, it is my preference to use the oh no you don't method of reality to resist their take over assault. If under attack-one of the Kurt Russell 'Escape From…' movies, he just shot the damn things. They're computers. Too bad they couldn't just use EMP that's even neater. Upgrade. it's a mind pain weapon. They blast you, inside. Ramped. Not a headache more like super ramped. Make helmets lined with copper sheet, molded to your head shape, light and easy and tinned with a nice coating of lead solder. You can add to it for comfort using nice cushy layering of tin foil inside for resting on your head and used a covering of black electrical tape. Then it is the pressing it tight against the areas they are attacking that cuts off the waves. Not the 'overall' oops what about your neck etc. it is the tight over where the waves are being aimed. One easy way is to take a nice large thick towel, wet it thoroughly in a bath tub to wrap all around your head, hug it up nice and tight centered midway at the base of your skull at the back of your head and wrap each end up nice and tight too one after the other and take both your hands and press them as tight as possible down to provide as nice and sealed and air tight fit as you can. Not hard. Just nice and snug is all. It can make a mess with the water flowing, so stand in the tub if you like, whatever makes you comfortable, and it will subside within moments, it's bearable. Water is a heavy substance and effective block. Our bodies are made up of mostly water. It insulates us. Very, they used water. Then got it handled that they even had to do that. How outrageous is that? Did you see those instructions? It is true crime and it reads like a movie plot. Now, listen up, they had secret psi, now turned back on our side as a weapons experiment. Yeah, right. That works. Not. Me I am just a messenger of one harmful circumstance. The Americans are entering into panic mode. It is their beloved country and patriotism is everything to them. That and the LORD. They are being terrorized for being American. Now, we Artists work all hours. No stranger to Night Hawking since people often interrupt in the daytime, with creative work you often get more done at night. Cuts the interference. When the Nasa goons are gone I will get some sleep. It's NASA BEING CRIMINAL BABIES ABOUT NOT OWNING SPACE. But not wanting anyone else to do anything or get credit either. They need to be fired, or the long arm of the law comes to mind. They won't even likely mention that AMAZON deleting files on personal computers, those ebooks they were selling on 'kinder' … a morning story, early Friday morning on a summer day. The media likely won't mention it again. //Recent Views are stupendous using Stargate 5th D capability, but like the Pentagon stealth use of RNM 'Telepathy" release…they would and some are intent on a methodology of - just bury it and don't mention it again. A bit like the former PM of Alberta, Klein and his 'shoot shovel and shut up' advise, his homespun version of making sense. Not taken too well by the rest of the tribe, it was mad cow disease he was on about. Not wise, leaders have to make like owls.

Operation Eastern Resolve II Afghanistan

US Marines shooting the door; View match to door, outlined in black dots

After shooting the door; View of troop with gun; excerpt from View painting prior to my gun course, showing a reversed so you can see it better, visual of open gun; RV open gun

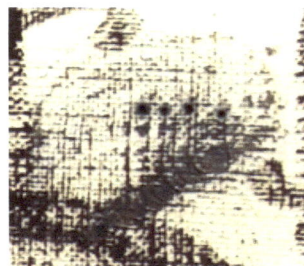

Taking down the door, Afghan.; dots over heads, match to RV (right).

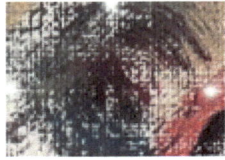

VIEW of a Wizard's tall hat; RV crystal ball

'1984' by George Orwell, about Big Brother taking over. I hear shredders…./The media will cover it over like an ocean to a drop of water. Count on it. They are responsible for all the atrocity currently happening. They made it so. This is the MEDIA MEDUSA the gorgon with snakes …the cables they use….they turn everything that looks at it to stone. our land from this invasion. There is not going to be any instant quiet Islamic enforcement. They need to get that understood.

"WAR IS PEACE - FREEDOM IS SLAVERY - IGNORANCE IS STRENGTH" '1984 ' by George Orwell, www.mondopolitico.com/library for the full book free download. Or from a 2nd hand book store. Make They can't 'just go buy it up' do you know how many second hand book stores there are in our lands? Do you know how. Bookworms for all! There is another source for them, garage sales. It's a classic they have them all over. They won't get rid of this one to save themselves and just casual glancing at it shows this is And (I already told you they were using it. It's in my book.) This is just proof. And right now, damn good tips as to their actions and aim…they're not joking. That Chestnut Tree is ACORN. And that story on tv, about them censoring it ouch will get people all running to check out what about the classic we all know it as. The Boomers will all go look it up. Lots of them. Readers do that. We look things up. They will. More and more will be reminded of it and wee what these clowns at the top are doing, too. They are showing like the tip of a worm being pulled up out of the ground by a bird.

They could be using Swine Flu to remove the elderly. Driven by Caste and Young, Holy Grail Islamic style. They think if they get rid of the Boomers who know the history of Earth and the old timers they can rewrite it. Hey, it's possible. Perhaps they don't want in the USA to pay for the old ones health care. Hey it crosses your mind. They have new 'provisions' and what the T party call 'death boards' on their new reformed health care program they're working on down in the States. What aims and intents? To erase our kind starting with the top down. Like they are using gas in chambers. Is it to be designer death and they can tweak it to kill whenever they want, an assault tool? Back to ye good old cave man bashing in of the fancy digital quantum RNM centers. Use all you got rules could be coming to town. Not a moment too soon. They could be doing some weird twist to the concept of boundless youth, a spin off from the Immortality theme of the Last Crusades legend in our heritage. These Anti Crusaders really dish it out too, heaping on the works, among them, stalking and participation in an illegal torture experiment. Damn. No wonder Will Smith's movies pre the American Congressional controls, are all so full of the Remote View themes. They broke it apart at 'Jumper ' and Smith's 'Hancock' was arranged. Not real Viewing, it was scripted carefully according to their own agenda. Using the old book '1984' and the Congress, our modern upgrade with computers, and the new white apes' triad. We have no freedom and their censorship is really unfamiliar to us, and it is every bit as lousy as you could imagine it would be.

//Head of DHS seemed ok for a while there. After the initial memo fiasco on Prophecy and Returning Troops as the New Terrorists. They sent it out to all the Law, then took it back, like bad children cursing. I think they keep her as their scape goat, one among others. She was nothing, a woman, and working hard to overcome. Seems she is another immune. And realization is clicking. As for the myth that their New Ruler 'cares' and is here 'for the people', watch the Tower buzz by using Air Force One shortly after he came into power. With Real Americans running into the streets as a result. Listen to the real tapes right after the event took place and listen to the tone of the new guy's voice, not this news guy, telling you how it is. The torture came next in order.

//They are hacking online and on personal computers like crazy these days. I am going for more flash, redundant for computer back up. American censorship forces to you, are now telling me where I can put my files on my personal home computer. We know they access by key stroke and it is more like what don't they access. But this is new, this is censorship and control. I already know our side is not going to like it. An invasion of our privacy and an attack on our Freedom. It's also an attack on our copyright laws and likely more than that even. Sacrificing our Freedom for Quiet is not something we all are in agreement on. Quite the contrary. //In full Argzoom Mode…leaving with a sense of our own bliss bliss, that sounds good to just continue to call it the *Stargate* and go with the name we all know …and relate to, and share 50/50. And I might add, that's legally ours. Nothing to do with these Communists.

//Team O is intent on destroying Capitalism in Canada as well as our Freedom. Online and off. Digitally and physically placing us under censorship. These schemers are likely upset their take on '1984' is exposed. No way our civilization will allow it. We Canadians love our Freedom ever so much. To those that know and those that caught that clip on tv today about how Big Brother is online into the electronic books and erasing them from personal computers. Totally unacceptable to us in terms of our normal freedom expectations. Our reality boxes. Prior to this new arranged statehood. More like hood winked really. Through our cultures' book worms, carried on as Views tend to do. View inspired tales and visuals. More people would have learned the truth about the ongoing turn of events down South of our border, just by going to their books and looking up that George Orwell piece. Surfacing to connect to other creative of classic literature. Looking it up and going, wow, the words on the first page…**BROTHER IS WATCHING YOU** Done years ago in huge bold dark letters. Views as such, surface to reveal their messages. Count on it. Viewing does that routinely. And we just don't live how these bastards do. In the book '1984' the main character's name is Winston Smith. Someone is listening. Winstons are also an American brand of cigarettes. They were up here, using their inserted into our lands ACORN now called Communities' Organizations International. Good thing we have soldiers to protect us. However far from home, the Military are on our side and working for our side. Learning they had a US major company, delete works off people's private personal computers using Amazon online, for cover is way over the line in terms of our societal decency. Big time. //Just tired. NASA is doing sleep deprivation techniques on us lately, in addition to their other atrocities.

//There is certain enemy getting in, who are after dismantling our system,

Democracy , Capitalism and our Freedom. Their intolerance is showing more and more as they prepare to attack, attempt to attack, and attack us. Since all these Anti Crusaders too, are Anti War they will be twice as horrified when they realize down the road that they have brought them another Revolution if not WWIII if not Armageddon here on North American soil. We will tear them apart. Yeah these monsters are not sane and not joking and our people will freak out on them when the truth becomes more realized and the populace more aware. They will freak right out….they might *make* the Military nuke them. No, really./.I didn't even bother to look at the new online article about saucers. With Nasa involved it 's all bs arrangement. Not worth wasting my time. I have just about had it we worked tirelessly for over 3 years saving lives for our side. You have the enemy set up inside you now. They are torturing us for saving lives on our side! How absurd is that. I object! We are going to Court! Some day, some way. They are the Anti Christ and abomination rolled into one. They are torturing and have done so horrendously previous to our screaming about it to the forces that know, and can insist on some controls, so now it is more manageable and not so blatantly ramped on hammering us into oblivion. They tried to remove the Stargate, And by so doing, stealing the youth's right to a progressed future. No Stargate, no interstellar friends, and neighbours, no Star Trail travel. Just their idea of improved Big Brother complete with forced labour camps for any groups with issues. Like complaining about the RNM assault weapon and not having our freedom like it was, you know, free before. You feel violated and defiled and they are happy campers. We may need Military rescue like they do in the land of Turkey. Where Islam often takes the vote. On the sly of course; they get bussed in, set up and take over. It's going on here, we're trying to warn and they are all in la la for love beads land. Should just print this and go out and toss it into the winds for the Hindus and Hutus to distribute by their hidden and glorious farting system. Their superior hind quarters. The truth is not one leader is going to announce this. It's the Jones and Smith 'MIB' factor. The regular humanity standing together for Freedom. And nice try, but it may be a citizens solution in the States, they're armed. However not such a given up here in the Great White North. Different rules apply. But they are now

pouring in over the border to trash the Bible and ....think of them as the great white Apes in Michael Crichton's 'Congo' and you would be close. They're into revenge and savagery not protocol and harmony.
/ They're taking Chiefs under RNM suasion. Our Security is tattered. That's a hell of a big book when they are inside trashing and hurting, intense pains and background terror repetition take over tapes, aimed at overwhelming our own Security, destroying trust, driving in wedges, splitting apart common decency. All designed from our worst nightmare scenarios, creatively speaking, in our lands. When the abusers, CIA in this case, under orders, using RNM as a weapon and control object not any harmless communication aid. There is no doubt. You will know it with utter certainty. You don't go 'gee My *self* seems a bit off', when you are immune to their 'suasion' and able to see and hear them, no matter how small or quietly they are running their packets inserted using emf computer digitally enhanced means. Psi with a boost. And like the Nasa diaper dolls trip has shown you all, this has a physiological part to it as applied. It is every bit like being aware of an outside or alien say, force entering into your 'inner' space and attempting to control and influence. We believe seriously that they are using the RNM to cause 'sending' of the uninformed and untrained or anything to do with the Immunity achieved by Viewers. RNM is not Remote Viewing, it is just the Viewer is also psi linked to the same waves, called RNM the ones operating the machines (that was the Pentagon's release, calling it Silent Talk, about the mental Telepathy enhanced using computers modern program. Make no mistake this is not involving Aliens of any kind. This is coming from Earth by Earthlings. Straight from NASA/CIA and the abuse that JAG took NSA and Ft. Meade to court over already for previous RNM abuse on a human. //I am just a citizen Remote Viewer and it is my entire function to warn of impending disaster- the enemy are intent on destroying our Civilization. I work as a Viewer. If you want to learn about Remote Viewing go to....many fine online sites with other Remote Viewers, on the methods of this Open Stargate; extreme deep black ops. Very deep black. Think Men In Black. That's essentially what Viewers do. The SpaceTimeLight Hypershift 5th D is revealed to us by Quantum Chromo Dynamics. This one is surfacing into the public view.

There is that more to your understanding? They didn't own us, not really. Only in their own minds. We were volunteers but Stargate is fully ours to Claim. No doubt part of why they paid to have me tortured. Life just is, here in Spy Ville. Now get it right. STARGATE is the official and exclusive Open Stargate enabled by the Psi of First Viewer 5ᵗʰ D. There are others, they can do their own Claiming. I stuck it out through conditions the Post Office would find deplorable. It is so. It is not Nasa's to Claim. I am not alone. I am isolated but not without outside communications. Think the spy in the mailbox. I rely on many Spies who work this as well. Big Brother is drooling.

/I am surfacing this circus to try to tell you, something you can get off any of them who were working our side for years and who are aware of these difficulties in our current Security conscious times. For one, the creeping *Sharia.* And they would have in times gone by, have said, no worries, we use the Military to remove threats to our civilization. Now, it is the modern times. A more 'save the Heinies bleep the people'? Is that any acceptable ideology for the safety of our wonderful democratic Freedom loving lands? Hardly. Hence, 'ones in the know' released all the pertinent details to the media. Who passed it on in their cable channels running script line at the bottom of their screen for all of us. All that was necessary for a substantial warning. I am not your Revolution. Check out the Americans! Under their new Censorship, and the tearing down of Christian customs and freedoms! But it is an illusion as ill formed and unsuccessful and doomed to eventual and now seems like as good a time as any, and certain failure. The good people, the citizens of America (we're next, toppling like dominoes, not going to take years), are Revolting. Wooden Walls an original Oracle warning, now surfacing into these Military link times, they were using them on the sides of the ships during the Civil War in America. This is the American Revolution II. If you are not being hoodwinked, but are tuned into current real time events. It's the aim and the consequence, and it is Patriotism and Freedom all the way. The disconnected are like the ones who know about Stargate and Bleep and I controlling it, and they're still all doing Mars and Nasa their way. Rejecting the Quantum Leap! This leap has already reached the other side of the gap folks. We are not doing Nasa. We gave them the boot. We are doing Stargate. Always were. We are ousting them from our discipline and legal enterprise. They are infringing on our copyrights and freedoms. They need to be stopped of course. Get it right, these days include Quantum phenomenon and this *is our Stargate*. We booted them. OUT. /They have trouble understanding. That's why they call it stalking, when the obsessed won't leave you alone. Or kidnapping is another term for it. They need to get over their rejection by me, and keep the bleep away! I tell them, "You are illegally on my anything. Mars is Claimed. If anyone wants to hear about it they can contact Stargate's owner, being the real open star gate, as the Viewer extraordinaire, who rode it out. And now on…." Basically, Nasa is trespassing on Mars now, only I like the Rovers Spirit and Opportunity so they are most welcome. I will discuss Nasa's littering habits with a lawyer sometime in the far, far future. //Here is a line excerpt from '1984' by George Orwell the same one Amazon raided personal computers over, to delete without permission files on peoples home computers. Saying they didn't have the right permission to publish it. So their new commie censorship solution, the Big Brother Way was to invade home computers and raid them. Delete files. Put money back into accounts, it was apparently a downloadable ebook arrangement. They just did. No rights to do so, they just did. One interested party is suing them of course. You fight for Freedom and Privacy. This same book they were compelled to erase in computers, is also available for free in its entirely online. Strange they had such ulterior agenda, strange it was the book '1984' Ayers the Anarchist and linked to bombings, good old Terrorist style, down in the USA. That Ayers, connected to the Weatherman and Team O. Well during his old book of his but new re-signing photo op, he referred to this same old revolutionary classic, coincidentally, eh? So Amazon dives into our files now at their whim and fancy, contrary to the rest of us and our preference to adhere to our normal Free Speech and Privacy! Obviously these old standbys were just *in their way*. And not a problem.

From '1984' Part One, Chapter One-

'inside the flat a fruity voice was reading out a list of figures which had something to do with the production of pig iron'

Reading the book on guns, learning gun talk. Interesting time link. \For the we need 'proof' of the real kind, here is a tip that was revealed to us about some physical evidence, that Nasa uses the RNM and does the 'abuse'. That Astronaut female drove 3000 miles to 'kill' some female and had diapers in the trunk. Means their handlers er, monitors were using it on them too. And Abusing the bleep out of it so what happens to NASA? Nothing. The female had to go to court over it but that's proof. They use the female's wetting themselves. In overseas countries females have animal rights. So they make they wet themselves like the animals they are as if you are not housetrained sort of. It was done somewhat differently to me, what don't they do to me...I was kinda happy planning my escape to whereabouts unknown. //I am trying to learn gun it is not easy. Under these circumstances. These are rich coke heads and other hard drugs working humans like puppets. Not just a few lone viewer kids for their mind farms. They are in at a few different angles and they are clearly using 1984 as their read along game plan, when they aren't twisting the Ark-esque here, playing Gods at the top. I saw that one on Star Trek. When I first started the Recon it was along with jpl.nasa.gov/Cruise-jewel-box was the pop up fax. Daily for years. Just sharing some previously secret ops details. //View of a knife (pg. 48) I did as practice to the movie 'Sahara' about adapting solar in the desert. I did the entire knife as a psi-chi unit. These painted Views are done with a rapid chi process that involves your ability to shift the 5th, and leave a complete encapsulated quantum recording using this chi application. A masterful painting process. All encoded, and decipherable, but Veiled as Revelation is, as well. With the odd great complete View Capsule coming through, the knife did cut a rope in the movie, as it shows next in this View painting, done as a complete visual unit, easily recognizable for the article it portrays. Done in a seriously rapid painting technique, not a movie special effects trip. No coloured flashing lights or anything. However the mind has so much unused potential this is obviously a trained and psi skilled ability that taps into that normally dormant facility existing within our individual selves already. //Our people are shoppers. They think they can go out and say, we want this and this and that over there and maybe some…to go with it. They are not prepared for any Revolution. So it is a good thing we have Security who can click into place at any time we all need them. And we all rely on it. Thinking about it really…but right now I am just glad for small mercies. And I can't wait until they are trying it on you all. They're insane, totally delusional they actually think they can …they 'won'. They're like nuts in Beverly Hills. //I am not expecting Real Saucers and Real Aliens to come popping up and start circling my home. Ninnys. For you to do so, and have the audacity to wake me up to re-see that guy's show about the 'real ones' flying around him, (there are many UFOers and the vast variety of Aliens) shows that you are still trying to force this Stargate to conform to sceptical Realists standards. Linear or nothing. The obviously don't know how to do those 2D repeat graphics to 3D wonder cards, by holding them up to your nose and pulling them slowly down at a slight angle. Here I will take the liberty to redisplay one such creation. They don't just magically appear. alien friends, of course there are Aliens in the Universe. And of course they are all over Elsewhere/when. Hold the above visual up to your nose and pull it away slowly, you vision can and will hook onto a 3D image and transform the viewing Window into a wondrously holistic experience (see example you can use to do one yourself on pg. 48).

Stargate and Remote Viewing involve immersion in the discipline, strict isolation, and hours that make work-aholics look lazy. Being a Remote Viewer also involves full time, that's right, 24/7 monitoring. Bye Bye to Privacy. Hello transparency. Comes at a high price, this wonder spy eye Leaper ability. You have to watch they don't get controlling our lives. This is not the Truman Show. We work counter terrorism and rescue attempts. When it is Mission Impossible anything goes. And it results in some truly fascinating glimpses into Spy Ville. As well as having Viewed many Light Years distant, astral traveling with a time kick. There is much to explore using Stargate. Many life forms, many ways, as many stars. And no, I was not nor am I expecting 'real aliens' to come winging by me. You are still wanting a Movie version. The Stealth in the movie is a creative visual, a View link. As such, these View links are often *descriptive in style, telling a story or revealing an info packet, this is after all Quantum Leap in the rare and raw* . Now, it doesn't mean that real Aliens couldn't drop us some real time messaging, perhaps via an open STARGATE Take this one for precedence, in our time's terms, then, owned and operated by Bleep and I. Exclusive rights to its MI and MIB endeavours. The Inquisition met the old Axe. //Go read up on how Viewing operates. The double z I tuned into was Aziz. We already got that. As for Aliens, they work psi too, I would imagine some anyway. There are links. And bonds of recognition. I won't say what else more I would have no idea, about aims and aspirations of Aliens. How 'bout you?

Remote View paintings by 1st 5th , 'Immersion' oil/canvas 2004; 'Mathland' 2005

Remote View - action movie 'Terminator Salvation'; (below) RV by 1st 5th

RV in 3D paint of black Space Ship in 'Terminator Salvation' movie; RV close up

The ship in the movie 'Stealth' was like RV. The Military Black ops of Stealth and then the surfacing here of the Stargate. All part of what RV is about. So, you have the Stealth movie and the View I did, prior to seeing the movie Stealth, as I do all my Views of the Movie links. Sometimes seems like aliens' connections to ships and Military. That's some or one or part of the descriptive. Also the Stealth as in black ops secrecy figures in and the Military connection is a reality and a given. I didn't just get online and start saying I was working an Open Stargate….

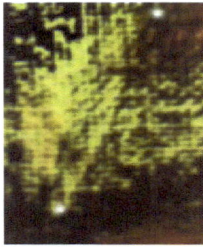

Views: author JAWS John A. West ; Knife cutting rope from Viewing, painting prior to seeing the movie, 'Sahara' with it's matching scene; ship, also painted using Military trained psi-chi; Velociraptor claw

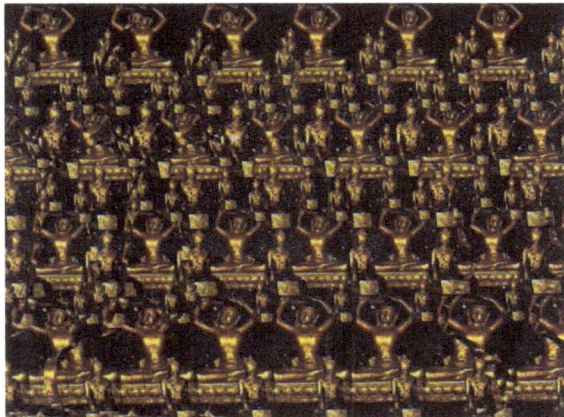

 3D image graphic; Requires instructions to unfold from 2D into 3D visuals; Like reading the 5th d, takes training & skill to render & decipher the emotes & descriptives of RV; (above right) tail end of 'Chariot', full papyrus near end of this book

View: US Air Force, the day they swooped the 9/11 World Trade Center spot in New York accompanying Air Force One, to redo the Terror; my authentic Australian whip Brings to mind images of ancient Pharaohs. Handy if they take events further.

Seemed like a good place to put up a note about our being separate from Nasa and their trip. Since in all reality we are. No I am not their prisoner. What part of Civil Liberties violation didn't you get? If you are still torturing and interfering with my freedom that would just make you the illegal holder, then a kidnapper, technically. No one can just take humans captive. Slavery in the US was abolished in 1865. //As for Open Stargate and my Alien(s) connection, I was certainly not expecting them to show up and not to me anyway! Those are your own ideas of what is happening here. Not what is really happening when Stargate is Open. Real Aliens could be already whizzing around his place and others anyway. Most likely that's for real. Are they tuning into Bleep and I? how would I know. Go ask them. They're Aliens. We do psi.; we View. We are already accomplished Viewers with tons of proof. We don't need to keep explaining to sceptics who have no right to keep making it so. Not only sceptics at Nasa they lie too. They already know about the Phoenix Lander Race and the real results. They want all of it to be them. And their other friends from respectable academia. As for your ridiculous Nasa XXXX, they also think the Hollywood movies are 'real' and 'a parallel universe' that is 'happening'. that's absurd. We don't go home and expect movies to happen either. I don't even want to see Nasa's pictures anymore of any outside space walks of Earth. I find them unrecoverable, they are duds. We gave them the boot, the large one. They're still here? Without permission? That's illegal. And they are doing a lot more than just loitering. They're falsely imprisoning, censoring, torturing, the list is long. That reminds me I have to find that list to talk to the lawyers later on. About what all these criminals are up to and causing me injury. And that's reality for you, our civilization's progress not their Idolatry. And that Phoenix was an example. During the honourable Smith and Jones MIB days we achieved a good deal of remarkable and astounding Views. I do have and I most likely do have 'alien' contacts, then if they want to come here to Rescue fine. Here to Earth. If they are already here and coming and going that would make sense too. And if there are some real Galactic Security Forces getting their tools of Planet Wipe ready for the days when it gets that there is nothing but criminal psi torturing an entire planet, and they need to wipe so it doesn't get into Space, then so be it. It is not my criminal psi tool it is the USA. I did my function as a Viewer. You have been warned. All you see is nothing done lately because you are interfering. This is not how it was done prior to the new guys taking control. We didn't spend all our time defending and being raped and writing weird books on torture. Check it out. Like white and black , day and night. No comparison. That's a reflection of their criminal actions against us. And the main reason we are now not with them, but they are stalking us, not letting us go, it's a 'civil liberties violation'. As in kidnapping they hold you, slavery they make you work. They see it as them upper Class Caste privilege, us bottom workers. Is it to be forced labour camps? That's their mind set and the reason for all the fuss now. That's why we are needing to surface this warning to others who are in positions to act as needed. At least make preparations. And if you don't want to read up on how this works, then just go away. At this point we don't want to tell you to do anything but just not be around us. Self Defence is also our right. Osama had the show of taking up arms, on the cable news they all use to chat nowadays. He was all flustered when they learned we were not just unarmed sheep. They're now not on the same firm footing they are goats on the side of a slippery ridge…instead of just breezing along on their silly cakewalk! //More aggravation. They have the printer messed up. It is new. Only a couple of months old. They have it hacked. It prints not what I put in to print it just does a collection of pages from all through the document random. It inserts a bs order. Not the 5 pages I wanted. It is their idea of 'not linear, the 5th) they're total baboons. //That's why the knife thing, and the lady clerks saying 'the guys buy them'. They don't want the females arming. They want it to be like overseas. They use RNM as a weapon. I am busy defending my self from the enemy Al Qaeda, their followers and sympathizers. They don't allow the females human rights. They don't want anything but their normal to them, horrendous to us, Sharia. No rights and certainly not armed. Must chill them to the bone, if their females armed. Well, it would be a different world over there. Their number one reason for the recent focus on 'cross dressing' and they like the word cross as Crusader theme imagery. So, guys if you are not interested in stopping them you will be looking at your wife's underwear with a whole new nudge nudge wink wink perspective if they keep going the way they are with the RNM abuse. Bet that shut them all up….//I found this very old drawing, I was 17 and a bit years old, I just met the first hubby there, it's his poem on the earliest drawing I have left and the paper was thin to begin with and I am mangling it with tape, so here….Some steps theme running through. The Mayans built Step Pyramids. Hope it is not the 'Apocalypto' theme by Mel. Could be. Could be RV (that's short for Remote Viewing). If it is, it is something to do with steps, signifying *linear* as well as *over the border, steps*. Also, multi linked as per usual with the View Themes, it is the pyramids/Mayan 5th age, and the Pirate's ladders. Ladders are a step, levels are a step, that's more of the 5th allusion, or reference that is. We are victims of political/religious persecution, in this day and age yet. And their arranged punishments. As well as many other trips all enemy, currently attacking the Security. They are using this torture weapon and their repeats, (Islamic art is repeats, not random creation as a descriptive of their overall mindset. That's real and it shows in their approach to things. Our civilization is greater because of our Creative abilities. We make, they take.) I say our side has the stronger winning solution. We make it to the Stars with Jesus guiding us. They would just get Planet Wipe if Mo takes it. And do my 'friends' get to send me a memo? I think they already did. //No they didn't. it's a matter of perception. They didn't 'win', they stole. My Archos of video clips was fried by their henchmen *before* the vote count on voting day, when I took the photo of the Black Panthers at the voting station. Their sneak preview of the censorship to come. They attacked me using a White House hired hacking team for months after. The Regime change was not a vote, it was a Coup; that didn't change. The truth and the light will win out over this darkness. With a bit of focus., /that mall I tromped through didn't have a lot of lumber in the new construction wing. I need to do up a real honest to goodness STARGATE card, viewer ID. This is the Stargate that preceded the movie. I will try that one. That's why they use the CIA and a tool if the spies want you buried you're buried only. Remote Viewing surfaces of its own accord. We are just along for the ride. Certain warning potential. Must be a psi species alarm mechanism seeded by the Creative Operative of the Universe. God is another name. No discovery is easy, a Star Trail is no different, it requires real travel time for exploration.

Step   pert : go out   m : IN

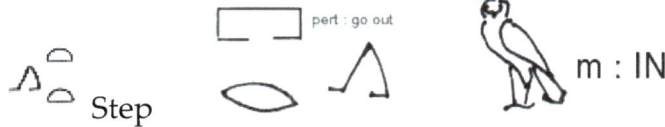

STARGATE BLASTING OFF burnt, tortured …Leaping into the Heavens; hieroglyph 'pert' to go out'; the Wizard is IN.

Top line reads 'to float above the madness' and I believe the scrolls on its back are spiral galaxies…this is an inter-system established psi linked talent. We are so far past 'questioning' if there are others out there it is frightening to hear the media still pretending that is in any way a valid question. And the color theme is time context lined, to Ed Dames again, the Red and Green. And no, project up your heiney blue book has nothing to do with the astronomical mathematical calculation of red and blue shift and intergalactic ethics. You need to get past dino ville. Upgrade or choke on your own dino dust. You're not going anywhere. Your 'space travel' is not happening. For several real and pertinent issues. Not with those guys mismanaging. And that's part of why we at Stargate ditched you. A note from a spiral Galaxy. Or perhaps and/or to another Spiral Galaxy. See the Planet? SEE THE PLANET GO BOOM? Could be descriptive of Psi rays. www.iahf.com/NSA/20010214.html Could be literal. And there are steps with range. And there is a square like a flag signals, waves are signals, navy for sonar, etc. the rnm. It is up in the top part of the Planet form. It is a square but the parallel sides are linked by a diagonal from top right corner to the bottom left corner. Easy an eagle or a phoenix reference showing inside the ram's horn, the extra reddish…could be weather related, could be the idea of global disaster, could be fema, could be the weather man Ayers and O deals, they do like with Chavez. They're anti Capitalism. Anti Security, and can you ever see it lately, in the crime patterns developing here in our lands. Good thing digital is far more rewarding and there are far too many wonderfully absorbing things on Earth for Earthlings to enjoy. if Jihad Joe Junior ever did try to start up over here? Simply, there is no contest between freedom & anarchy.

'First Blood' movie starring Sylvester Stallone; RV his face, lower right corner & up side

There is an extra level with its own components. That's the descriptive and the actual link to the 5th D and discernable to other Viewers and followers of this phenomenal psi discipline. We train for years. Immersed and isolated, in Deep Black and reading codes and connecting visuals. It is time consuming, make that life consuming. Well worth the time tunnel ride. Exploration is both difficult and rewarding.

Viewers or Oracles as they were called and consulted, wrote as well. The scribe was also in the Christian church the maker of their illuminated manuscript visuals. I think as a society we are suffering a disconnect, a lost connection. The Edgar Cayce message under the Sphinx. There is a faction jealous and telling lies about this Remote Viewing enterprise. Of course, there are always critics and sceptics, these are just in overdrive about Open Stargate and the View's linguistic connections to ancient Egyptian hieroglyphs. They're trying, but Stargate is a Time Tunnel. It works! We already know it works this fact is not in question. It is not a replacement nor a patch for Death. No immortality pill. However, it's essence is extremely Time related. Timely enough I am currently trying to surface from the depths, this modern marvel. Open Stargate is very real, timely, decipherable and insightful. The security who access it for tips and back up, for years past, already know that. It is not a secret to us or to them, just to the new guys and general public. Surfacing it now for the progress and development of the hyper- shift. Also, in order to acknowledge and share with others the faster than light speed, hyper shift enabling of the 5th D. The 5TH is curved like spacetime. As a Viewer I experience it as attached to spacetime and more accurate and inclusive to call this *SpaceTimeLight*. Merged not separate forces at all. Most of us celebrate discoveries of this magnitude. Anyone still not with it, could just be they are anti our ways, anti Crusades and enemy. There is no reasoning. Good thing for the Remote Viewing in all its fascination. I had to do the movie visual practice first, to get paintings happening to learn the corresponding parts to apply the words to. This is based on quantum chromo dynamics, and are by nature audio & visual. Shows in arts. The Eye and the Ear are the connections. They are on the ceiling of the Roslyn Chapel. I found these as significant 'orbs' the storybook da vinci code was looking for too.

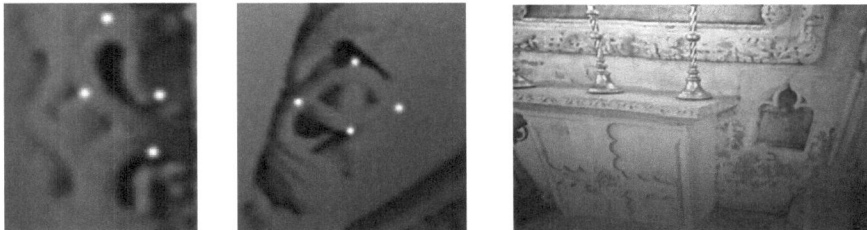

Carvings on ceiling of the Rosslyn Chapel; ear, eye, cross, orb themes

We don't know there are not life forms that are trying to tell you to turn off the RNM waves; you all carrying on in old Star Trek days mode. Since they now have special teams to perpetrate the RNM abuse it seems only common sense we need special teams to counter them! Psi is waves but waves or tools, the assault useage is still an *act*. In order to be properly responsible and ultimately successful. Of course. Freedom of eyes and ears. Necessary of course, for Open Stargate's responsibility to hunt for possible threats from hostile Aliens. Some of them with guns that do go

ZAP. Don't wait until they are on the doorsteps and go, *"hey look!"*. Survival with quality of life, the aim, not mind worm slave farms. RV is often psi sense as well as *ear and eye descriptives.* Viewing is what you do while immersed IN the Time Tunnel. You View. You do not 'do' you 'View'. Hence psi cast to one another our link. We go far far out into Space. //August 2, 2009 Turns out it truly was a Ghost. Navy pilot Capt. Scott Speicher turned up after a week of digging in the desert, missing for 18 years, since the Gulf War in 1991. Here is the View among other things I was picking up on, over his being found. I often did tune into the 'carve my words' they had found his initials carved into a wall some time back. And I do tune into the odd Ghost, especially Military. Pvt. Fouty went missing himself, captured by the enemy near Mahmoudiya in Iraq in 2007. The same *pointing* time frame from earlier. As for tuning into Military ghosts, or them tuning into me, rather, believing it is not hard. Folks used to be more tuned into their own psi and the 5th is a natural. There was a twist along the way, and it is now being rediscovered as part of natural Earthly phenomena.

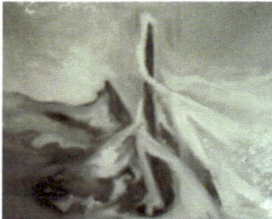

Pat Tillman passing on with purpose; USS NY made from Sept. 11, 2001 Tower terror attacks

'Witchcraft Act' (1541) "thou shalt not suffer a witch to live" to deal with fear and superstition. This misguided death penalty was abolished in 1735. Whew. The last person convicted was one Jane Rebecca Yorke, a medium apparently fined the sum of 5lbs no doubt staggering back then, for claiming to be able to *contact dead service men.* (1944).

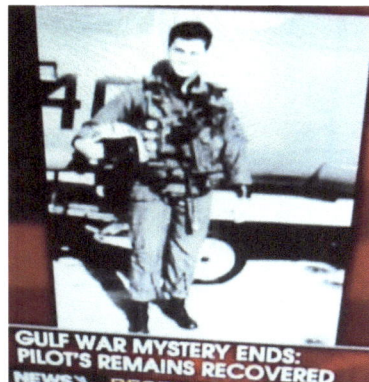

US Navy Pilot Captain Scott Speicher

(Left) I helped locate Capt. Speicher in this Iraqis desert, where the Bedouins buried him, he died the first night of the first Gulf War. Dug up by searching troops digging for a week, 18 years after he went missing; VIEW of photo above, helmet as a round form near the center; with an RV empathically sensed or emoted stick-man in the inner curve, holding a helmet; (right) Viewed number 4 match to the one showing behind him.

View of Cpt. Speicher, visual components match to photo at left.

Corporal Christian Bobbitt -a Canadian soldier who died fighting within this same time context when the Ghost of the Navy Pilot surfaced his joking spirit tagged along too. 2009

 A)  B)  C)

A) Spc. Alex Jimenez (left) and Pvt. Byron Fouty (right) missing in Iraq since 2007; presumed Ghostly contact by Stargate link; Pointing the way during the search for the missing soldier in Afghanistan, as ghosts have been known to do; they are together
B) his X shoulder patch
C) Chariot papyrus excerpt, an RV 'tower' theme, visually symbolic of 'hostage'.

We just cruise around at our own weird pace usually and accomplish many and various assorted wonders via Elsewhere/when. Those other clowns and nay sayers were only trashing it and turning this into some horrific nightmare experience. No kidding. It's the same as the psi cast now RNM mass with Abuse. Stargate is not a producer of miracles, this is their *Truman Show*. They have the dials. We have to figure out what to do. I say, don't worry the Military are always, 3 steps ahead. I usually indulge in as much work on Stargate matters as I can. I am hunting interstellar permits and here they are doing every blunder there is here on Earth to the point of full Planet wipe fears! Now get it right. The Galaxy is not an idle invention. Folks, this is reality. Viewers function as Reconnaissance, nailed to the front, to give warning and aid in Rescue and other exotic missions of an impossible nature, should we so chose to take them on. Sometimes, in fact most times lately it is overwhelming for happenings. Tired of warning you, so bye and have a nice mind wipe. The rest of us took the 'other pill'. Here's a tip, don't hang your large raw meat cut for the day outdoors for too long…in case of large snarling hungry man eating cats….just saying…

Remote Viewing

Melbourne, Australia '09 Terrorist round up

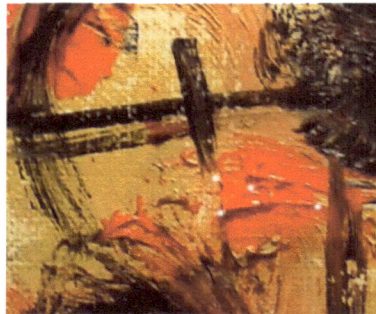

Remote View Canadian RCMP Musical ride; RCMP Red Flag RV (in dots); RV bullet

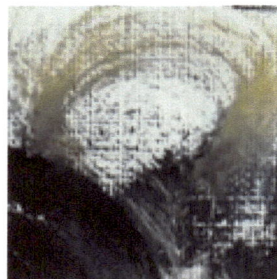

Afghanistan 2009; View helmet wrap

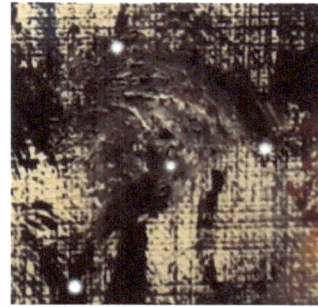

RV 'Pliosaur' streak outlined in white dots; the same Pliosaur shapes appear in the View painting (above, right)

RV emote- 'Pliosaur'; RV emote- long necked dinosaur emote and remote View showing top 'looks like a spiny ridge'; between dots; grey form

RV 'Pteranodon Ingens' a type of Pterodactyl; match to Navajo Code Talkers of WW2 fame; they said 'they'ld have liked me better if I was Haitian' in time code….

//Like any good view does so often, Stargate is officially surfaced-ing. I say yes they say no, I say heave they say ho... I think they should send most of the security to one of those space-ship fields of dreams and do visual training. Good for 'wow, wonder what it is? Keep the old open minded get ready for Quantum Leap ...on track. The aim of our imagination and creativity.

A thought experiment- take a whole bunch of money and an empty operations base and call them Stargate and send in Nasa and all their experts and specialists minus the Viewers. Take another team of just the two Stargate Viewing Ops currently occurring. Give them paint supplies, spy cameras, laptops and a good color tv. Then see which team produces Views, interpretation and copyright. Why we have Stargate not them. Here I will go operate the Real Stargate, going to paint...this coming off my personal computer environment and here that is mine only. Any further interface is entire on your side and accessing this material of my own creation. I am not under any voluntary or contractual or legal requirement to satisfy or link to another human whatsoever except for the other Stargate operator, Bleep. That's how Open Stargate functions. We work MI, we select and we have total free reign we serve no master other than the usual, the Lord. There is not to be any outside tampering and interference with any ark-esque and you are forewarned of your own peril if you chose to do so. I are busy, we work Security functions Viewing the front. We are only sidetracking to surface this wonderful 5th showcase of wonders to share with the rest of our creative civilization. As to any warning tagged along, hey, it's MIB there is always something going on...it's just Earth. And you need to stay modern. At a new quantum pace guys. They passed Newton back that a way. This is a whole new era already operating. Like Stealth & Area 51 finally being revealed to the Public audience. They want a go at a real Stargate. Something pointing the way. As bad as we do. The ones doing this solitary ride into the stars. It isn't easy. But you have to make the Leap ...lots of us already have in our modern society. Wow spy stories. The British Secret Service with bad guys in among their own. Infiltrated. Implants, imposters, 'sympathizers' call them what you will. They're helping the other side! And the rest is just in terms of 'degrees'...another descriptive to the compass rose. Roslyn very

Place and Time specific. Fascinating. Very Spock. Very logical. //No be sure to make that distinction it is not 'helping' if it is being milked like a lab rat specimen with no rights and only punishment. Make that certain discernment. One is turn coat the other is victim. //it was the Army shot up the first rocket into space wards….I don't remember what they called it. Seems to me that signs that they likely do make it to another planet to explore, from the ground. Then next big Leap for Sol 3. Oh, I see…Sol 3…way cool and let's not trash your permission to access our Viewing. You see it because of us. *Stop spitting on the window.* You have to tell them everything.

Oh they want a new one. Gosh not sure how I got that one I was just banging on a key. Or something and voila. Like Open Stargate eh? Oh the French yeah I gave them a raw deal eh? I have nothing against them. I was just taking back a bit of the blanket if you don't mind. This of course turns out to be a pre-courser to a ghost. Read on…Stargate surfaces. That's better. Captures the spirit more. Open Stargate is well worth the experience. Sorry, we were spying on Al Qaeda etc. And not telling anyone or showing it to any. We were working *deep black* secret ops. That was then and this is now. We are surfacing this into the light of day, for all. We are not staying *deep black* since they started abusing with RNM. They started using RNM=Psi link as a weapon. The problem is not Stargate or psi, not us, it is the RNM being abused! The Pentagon released scant details. This is a super bad development. They are in and they are. We in security doing *deep black* ops we work with *deep black* as well as the rest of the. It's a secretive world. We are not the weapon. The prior JAG trial about the NSA and CIA and NRO (that's the National Reconnaissance Organization) they take you as Recon. The Military etc. whatever it's recon you nail your self to the front. We're nailed out front in a dreadful Islamic Holy War. …so, the Military has View Trainers. It takes two gruelling years. Sleeping wet doesn't sound all that …never mind. I say lots of things I don't mean. that's ok they …never mind. Life as a Viewer. It's all spy all the time. If we had lighting up boards the room would be full. It's a riot. And we have to try to save and rescue and not a single memo shoved up my butt. We work constantly I am not complaining. Well I do, but not right now. I get a certain amount of gloating time. Hey, it's a room. We work we earn it. So Gov. Schwarzenegger, today I couldn't spell his name. Total Recall. I am trying to spell his name. must be something up. I always spell his name right. No it is not the marijuana I am spelling all the other words fine. We read the slips as code. You have to be able to read along. It's a language that develops on its own and is psi time code linked. We play in the time tunnel. We don't get out much. We're busy. But now these mean take over crew are …it's not ignorable any more. They're setting up and using RNM to lull the populace starting top. The enemy busy trying to set up their tents! Stargate is challenging enough, just using Psi link and did you catch that? In the Open Stargate SpaceTimeLight tunnel, psychic Viewers are mostly happy campers, wizzing along in hyper shift 5ᵗʰ, Viewing remote distances forwards and backwards to the future and into the past. In terms of application mostly we are reading forwards for the survival of our humanitarian civilization, hence the certain focus on the War. Like Delphi, this is a Military Oracle. However we read Future trails and we track looking to rescue too. If you get lost on an isolated mountain top, or overboard at sea, for just a couple of examples, Bleep and I using Stargate Views, sometimes painted the day before an event, sometimes the day after, determined by psi with certain givens with priority status, join in the search for you. Providing clues, tips and descriptions. The one dot leads to more, and two dots points in a direction, we comb for. But I get off on weird trails too. Don't expect to like see me, if you get lost. It is necessary to make sure they don't waste time and energy doing an Inquisition on Open Stargate. Already overwhelmed these days. Signs and behind the scenes knowledge of RNM abusers, abusing, twisting our psi-link as if it is dangerous. Only, it is them with the damn controls and wave ramping and subliminal reinforcement and who knows what all else these modern

digital morphs quantum days. They have this computer enhanced ability under their control, for one. It's a wave length emf I think, the details are in the online material on the old RNM JAG case. Remember the old Stealth flying craft? And area 51? They all knew it was there but no one was talking? We are the next one. And if you watch the movie 'Stealth' they actually mention not me, the Stargate and Viewing. He says if you are quick to hear it, around the Stealth craft as they first walk around it, he says, he would get paid if only he could learn to connect the dots. The great rip off, 'if only they could connect the dots', is great for cover story, they like to say that it is not working while undercover for secrecy and protection. However, then the powers that be, use it as a set up to not pay anything, keeping it Officially- *on the shelf*. While I work as an unpaid slave, day in and day out, hours only a mad man would preside over. Open Stargate really needs decent funding for it's research and development. The potential is staggering. That's the Viewer *paid,* not the way they do it now, like a miserable unfunded inadequately assessed and supplied, meagre paupers sillyness they get to avail themselves of; Whips out in full Pharaohs' Slave mode! Apparently you go in the time tunnel. That's that. We are Stealth. The next generation of spy craft. So, of course, speaking for myself, I was taken and thrown into the middle of an Al Qaeda Shiite bloodbath carnage in Baghdad, Iraq while training. Full time, no time off, goodbye privacy and freedom, hello 'assisting' …but no credit and no pay! I am attempting the Moonlight Lemons here, but hey the Views are great. Still, where is the credit and/or the pay?
 Fascinating. I came in as accomplished, I had already painted the Planet Mars solo, as a great View and subsequent Planet Claim. I linked two flag paints, precision oriented around a particular jump point, a certain specific rock, confirmed as linked to twice, two separate Jumps. 'Total Recall' enabled, confirmed by two separate Jumps or Views of Mars, both times from the same identical rock. Once, done as a 'water on this world' Viewing descriptive, and over that many years later, a complete over lay of the actual View of the scenery in front of that same rock. The Nasa Rover's took photos that confirmed the actual match. I painted the first View and then years later when I heard the Rover Spirit was glitching and the Rover Opportunity was only then on its way to the surface, I

decided to do a painting and race it down. This time I painted Mars as the real surface new in front of that same rock. So, it was my two different jumps prior to the Nasa Rovers reaching the surface to explore territory and perhaps stake Claim. However my Views were completed previous to their arrival and I chose to lay Claim, signed copy at NASA and the Pentagon as per recorded. I laid this claim using the View rock in Endurance Crater. I did it in the foreground in the painting 'Face On Mars'.

//Then there are the flag paintings. This interesting tid bit is the ancient Egyptian hieroglyph View meaning Lord, a pennant. It was cosmically found as a match under the later NASA Phoenix Lander as a wee patch of water ice. Views link over vast periods of SpaceTimeLight.

There is a wee jag in that foreground Claim rock that I used both times, that we confirmed as a visual precision match to the one on Mars in that very place. X marks the spot is entirely possible with Remote View. And the bottom selection of rocks is of the jump rock and what you could see in the surrounding area. They were the actual match to the photos that the Rover took later on in time, when it got there. I beat them to that location and I used the same claim rock (inspired by the Marines planting a flag after toppling Saddam and the Tom Cruise movie 'Far and Away' where they do the Race for land. So I Claimed Mars. All outlined in full detail in the book 'Remote Viewing: Knights of Mars'. All fair and square. I have the two paints as the Flag. they are my Official Markers under Psi. I then took Sovereignty and Claimed it for the Knights of Mars that's the Military and coalition, Law Enforcement, Rescuers, and the Stargate past and present Remote Viewers. The Head Knights if you will, the co-equal share owners are non other than, California Governor Arnold Schwarzenegger & Tom Cruise & Kevin Costner & Bruce Willis! Signed with copies at Pentagon/NASA/Law In the spirit of adventure into Deepside & beyond.

Old View, first Claim paint of Mars 1998; (right) repainted in 2004 with surface View match to claim rock; Mars photo taken by Rover Opportunity 2004; Linked Claim rocks

Surface photo   'Claim' rock, RV match painted in 1998

neter : God

henety sh neter: one before divine boothe

5th Upgraded to: 1st in line TT

Flags in ice found under the Phoenix Lander on Mars; ancient hieroglyph for God, the line next to it indicates one; another fascinating hieroglyph, TT for Time Tunnel

For contributing to the effort although unbeknownst to them, with View links to act as lights, guides along my way to this accomplishment. Discerned through their creative works and attuned selections. I have in that previous book, named specifically the movies they got the special recognition and share, for. They did about two each, it's in the book anyway. Also in that book, is how I psi raced the Phoenix Lander to the surface of Mars. I got the exact view match and I had a View paint of precision links to the ice patch they landed on and the views were also visually linked to the Ancient Egyptians. Definitely, they had a time tunnel too. Graham Hancock has an academic book out on it. They found it at the Sphinx. Read his books. They're absolutely fascinating and entirely correct. Only Bleep actually found how to work one. Stargate is a real Star Trail. The Chariot papyrus is a Star Map using the 5ᵗʰ the Ancient Egyptian Viewers were masters. Absolute masters. They also had a heck of a lot less clutter and pebbles and RNM weapons. Anyway I use it, too. I read it. Drives the enemy mad. Seems bad guys had their mits on this counter terror window way back. Islam Rules, they started bragging. They are setting up to fight. Islam and the Anti Crusaders VS the Crusaders, that's whether you want to play along or not. The Crusaders are considered to be English Christian, Military and our Security forces. What can I do? Pass on alerts about ice berg tips when they're sighted. So, stop slamming the messengers, and maybe realize this is a good time to start checking out the warning we are knocking ourselves out trying to pass along about the RNM center abuse. The purpose of this book is to share some of the wondrous Views along the trail. As well as to make it official that Bleep and I are announcing this, our Open Stargate. Exploring the 5th D and it's Hyper-shift, I also managed to come up with odd but worthy life saving ideas. I actually get to share credit for coming up with and ragging into place a couple of doozies. Working full time since Feb. 2006. I was working lately on a case here where I live regarding them coming over the border and causing mass murder/martyr in a town called Smith. I assist with tips for the Law and the Military as well as Rescue. I have many accomplished views, I am also credited with the advisement of the covers they put up over the tanks during the War in Iraq, early 2006 and recently the Nato/coalition testing of a laser device to go ahead of the vehicles to detect buried IED explosives. And more. That covering was …also with this part 2. The sport gallery of their African Continent predators. You used Predator Drones. Oh boy. Now we get 'Predator 2'. That's ok, don't panic. They just have a Mind Control, or Telepathy-Out-of-Control, if you prefer, with certain methodology they can use to assert themselves and their wishes onto you. Abused, it is ramped to become so controlling as to be nothing less than an invasion. But no one who is uninformed (or like us Immunes) can see or hear or knows anything about it. An invisible largely undetectable tool meant to overrule freedom in a manner so complete and so insidious, it is no different than their entering into our personal digital spaces and deleting and inserting and trashing at will. Big Brother is digitally enhanced, attacking and censoring. One objective only, and that is to achieve world domination. Sounds mad? Don't look at me, not my mind control, er Telepathy they're ramping to harm humans with. Anyway from my position here of being nailed to the front, I can tell you not to just ignore this advice. They're here. They're setting up. The good the bad and the holy crap…if you wait you better bleeping well have wings to get you back here. And you better get someone with some authority to start getting your response team together …they're mostly trying, I repeat, *trying* as in not succeeding, with attempting some ridiculous notion of Sharia enforcement. These good folk have no idea what that is ….and right now they are testing the waters with mob styled community organized and …would you start sounding some Silent Alarms….look ahead, we are nailed out here for a reason. We tell them what's on the horizon. We also help watch and catch the Missiles and other cool shit that go way up…anti missile things that go boom into drifting out space debris. The satellites. I have that in my book 'Remote Viewing: Knights Of Mars' too.. (Nasa was told to not litter on my planet. They were already hurting me whenever they were up. I firmly believe they as in Bad Guys are using RNM to set up mass murder. Thing is to prove it. They are already using it. They send them to murder police and military and innocent civilians. They get them to mass murder and then suicide if you were overseas you would see it called mass murder martyrdom. After all it is Counter Terrorism we do here. And when they paid to torture they used the Enemy of our side. So they sold us to the enemy and we were there so we spy on them …under torture. They removed your security. Basically. So, as a result Bleep and I are with the understanding of the Navies surfacing a previously deep black ops. We don't get paid. I bitch. They tortured. They paid themselves to torture and they are not letting me get paid by writing about it. They could torture, and use tax payers dollars to do it, and that's not the worst of it. They are using the CIA under the new by Obama Leon Panetta to set up the Transportation dept to arrange for study of murder by train. They're serial mad killers. We work with the cops and the military any of them attacking us are considered under RNM …not everyone is under their subs controls. The computer RNM used abusively and now ramped to be an assault invasion weapon, on others. IF others were invading us…. sending in recon to set up and the photos are showing South Africa and Somalia. The War ships are in the Horn of Africa. Perhaps mad about the Pirates meeting their fitting ends, and our resistance to their violence and hostage taking penalties. Pirates, Islam, they're all linked, that's deliberate propaganda they are all running on separate ideology and aim. However that said, there are some indications lately that the youth may be digitally linking and liking modern and Star Trails not the doom the dinosaurs are trying to pass off on us. Digital and Spies working online so much , it comes with it's own occupational hazards. We are well aware at this point that our script work is accessed by them at will . That's the other side, in real time. Computers enable the crossing of the great divide, distance, as well as creating a chasm the un-digitalized have yet to bridge. Here in Stargate, we are busy and then some. We do as minimal other activities and dailies like chores and exercise as possible. We live the life of immersed monks, struggling to find enough time for our focus. Reading and interpreting and linking Views is vastly more time consuming than the under four minutes it takes to paint an 8" x 10" Stargate daily View for Security to do the piranha on. There is one Viewer calls himself the American Monk. We are the new Stealth some heard of but you are all just learning now. We are coming up, there is a security nightmare coming in. it's like being down below in water, with a giant prehistoric shark C. Megalodon and no cage. We get the bends coming up so fast. Pretty much. You run into trouble with sceptics etc. and they are running RNM abused without them even knowing it, that's the crime too, eh, they need to be hearing or seeing some action happening to make …it the security we all know and need. I walk …and it will keep the evil paparazzi back. Ok, wow. Stargate. Bet Bleep tells it way different. They do the Military view. I do look there's a hole on Mars! Take tourist photos! And I am trying to learn some gun parts. I think I am doing pretty good. on the learn guns. We are mostly rescue. The Military and intel spies and law organizations do their own decoding. They show us neat entirely . timely and relevant articles sometimes. And I find things like that cool Solar is great Sahara movie. I did the knife cutting the rope. I do great knives and blades. Lots of them. I also do a really great Harrison Ford movies Amazon blow gun dart. You throw one, and my psi vision will capture it to paint. Some of my other Remote Viewing books are filled with great Views. Viewers are immersed in it. Totally absorbed. Tunnelled. Anyway, we got warning from the Pentagon and are passing the results of our nailed out front as MI(B) spies. We do the jobs we are drawn to. No one but us controls the Stargate. These guys are not our side and they are torturing us and enemy and taking control and no one controls us. They got the boot. You all need to get up to speed. Your citizens are beginning to freak out. Too. With the strata they are seeing being pulled down around them. They're adding to us to warn you to get some serious response to protect our freedoms, happening. We have Enemy in and intent on taking us down……and CDIP is very real. Mostly time spent passing on impressions, doing readings, typing in script like this actually, to look for tips, linking in time context to the security issues and possible concerns facing our fast paced society. No time to not look ahead. As for new technological advances and research being turned and twisted as a certain violation of our norms and rights, this *is* the warning. Rather like passing along a message as a special Mission Impossible task. Good thing the Military are always 3 steps ahead of us all. Always. We count on them for our protection. That's what Warriors are for. The Police are also a serious target of these community attack forces. That's overseas and over here. They're not going to *not* attack, now it is showing Jihad is here, for real. Make your decisions. No one cares what they want at the top. The uppers tried 3 times to kill me in less than a week, using ramped RNM. One way is the severe attack on your head, a vicious mind wave assault. Use the helmet and the heavy fully soaked towel back of the skull covering turban wrap. The other was an accelerated heart beat. I have those covered. I have no vehicle and I walk everywhere regularly. My cardiovascular thought it was just a good work out. Lucky me. It's still a real trip and you have to tell your mind to calm it down as good as you can. Relax to counter it. Realize it for the temporary event it is. Your mind body control kick in and disrupt it's signal. That's basically what you are striving for. Bet there are a lot of immune among the martial arts disciplines. Heaps of them. That's why it is an attempted take over, in process. Not an accomplished fact. Not at all. We the North Americans are spit polishing. If I don't get that gun course, I will get a nasty dog and shine his teeth. And a large man with a larger gun. Preparation, fill extra water containers. Main priority is to attempt to sound alarms, and clang the gongs. Warn citizens so we all know what's about and being used, about RNM being real wow, and abused, ouch. We are only messengers. It's not my bleeping snarl blink blink computer doing the RNM and abusing it. They were taken to court by JAG at Fort

Meade, Maryland, D. C. (that's congress, we already know it.) that's a Given. Here in Holy bleep these guys had enemy in torturing us. You don't get that wrong. …all we do is spy for our side! We view like a Hubble telescope or a google Earth. Like that. Our techniques are computer linked and pixelated. To the point of madness, we train and train and to do this requires intense lifelong commitment. Bleep is famous for his Remote View of Jupiter in 1973. That's Time Tunnel for you, as he developed this Stargate. A thoroughly engaging process in itself. In fact it is so all consuming, in days of yore when they paid Oracles in emeralds they were tended to. Not 'tortured' my how things change. They are misusing it and …you have to do something rather fast. Whatever it is I would not have any idea. I tell them to nuke the enemy lots, for years. Sometimes they do, not because I say so. Just because they are there and nasty. They do horrible shit. We really don't want Jihad and RNM in these our, yes, *our* communities. They just called the cops stupid and then arranged to have the media look like the Mob paid them. As if they own them as their own pit bulls. The current slant to the show being allowed and arranged out. That and more. That's ok. Wait until….it is not one or any one of any one thing. It is many ways and we the ones used to dealing with them overseas. We Viewers did Iraq and Afghanistan for the works, in the air, the water the cracks the dark the fog the…you name it. We did it. We View. And I am tired and they are pulling in to slaughter and destroy. We all need some serious heed to this Pentagon warning they released, as I covered in the book 'Raw'. The bad guy's combo is too much. The economic woes is just about the least of our worries the way they are flooding in up here with attitude and intent, Sharia on the puppet Master's minds. That's what they are doing. Don't look at Stargate, for blame or rescue. What we do is recon and report. We go way out front, nail ourselves to the fronts of the ships and come back and Report and we spend most of our time almost always, doing Viewing sorting, linking associating as well as lots of practice Viewing. We are fine, Stargate being what it is. As spy eyes, we get codes. We don't get memos on how to do everything. I tried. We often do strange things too. It's the Time Tunnel effect. So, we laugh. I know Bleep does to. I have nice horrible hard hiking mountain boots for it the shit hit's the fan, but why clomp around they're heavy things too. Make them read this work or at least scroll through before they all start slamming Stargate as not working. It's their own overblown linear expectations that are not working. And we are just passing on a warning. You're lucky I am bothering. It's not my anything. We are the victims of their abuse. Let it be known this Stargate is alive and well! Call it this one in English, for the rightful Claiming of Mars for the Knights of Mars. As by virtue of psi Viewing it was claimed and presented as such for the Canadian, US and coalition Military, Law Enforcement, Rescuers and the seriously talented Viewers. Including of course, along with the Knights presented in the book 'Remote Viewing: Knights of Mars', namely Tom Cruise, Kevin Costner, Gov. Arnold Schwarzenegger and Bruce Willis; all co-owners, as detailed in the aforementioned book. Hey, the 5th D works. See further explanation in 'RV: Ancient Links & Future Trails' And yes it is spacetime with light attached. Our base is *Spacetimelight*. Psi via the 5th D, Given: v>c All bent like a bow. Do the fancy math using Quantum science mathematicians. CERN could handle it. That's where computers were first developed into the internet. I do Viewing. See 'Imaged 012' written super raw many years ago for more on the visual tips re the 5th. Here I have chosen to use clips of interpretation as translated in terms of the 5th and the Star Trail instructions, found in the Chariot papyrus. As for the Wizards View theme, I believe cops are Wizards. They often exhibit impeccable timing. The Military has a different Wizardly wave running through their own Elsewhere /when, they are more fully immersed in the 5th itself. You can see it in the papyrus and the ancient Egyptian hieroglyphs. They time link to other Military over the ages. Watching the View themes unfold is truly fascinating. Like their own timelight essence dip, they use to guide them along the way to the certain Star Trail. Stargate covers Deepside Views too. The handlers tether us to help Earth. I used to do Mars for vacation. Exploring. I spent years with Psi doing Mars. Very sensitive. And it was 'Total Recall' how is achieved the Claim Rock identical one both paints, the Flag markers. I went to the same rock on the Planet both Jumps. It was a righteous Claim. I signed it and they all have copy and now I have it secret. As the spy. It can surface as I wish. Or not it is on record. Kevin Costner is the human form I painted onto the surface of the planet Mars, in that Claim painting,

'Face on Mars'. See 'RV: Knights of Mars'. Kevin Costner was recently credited with helping to save people during a high wind event in Camrose, Alberta, Canada. The stage collapsed at an outdoor summer music festival, where his music group was playing. He displayed an honourable spirit that went past his own importance as a big Star, when he helped to rescue. Most worthy of inclusion, a Knight of the Planet Mars. Adventure and exploration require such heart and soul, showing in their concern for the well being of others. Along with a taste for adventure, it also took a precise Wizardly timing for the Phoenix Lander Race. I like to Race with psi against the others' mechanical visitors to the surface of Mars. I give them a fair head start. I can go to and from Mars with the real time View to prove it with them watching,…to and from Mars in under 4 minutes! That works out to faster than the speed of light and is incontestable. The participants of this Stargate all know and have the physical evidence and experience of that occasion. Far from imaginary, this Stargate View accomplishment is very real. I waited until they were at the descending to Mars or approaching it stage. But I still beat them. When I decide to Race them, I do it right as they are approaching. I really *Race* them. And Psi won the Race, hands down. We win. That no sooner said than the former rulers, now cut free, are seen by our spy eye to be fabricating around us. Reading our warning, and going for the opposite of revealing it. They chose secrecy and making sure there is no hurry back here, response. Targeting the most obvious link in the travel chain- Airbuses. Making sure, double cosmic coincidences. How nice and packaged. We work for the dots, they are not a list. This is not a linear system. They don't get that. //While everyone else is trashing and burying it, Stargate is claimed operated and surfacing. They forfeited it out of sheer inhuman indecency. They did chat on it when I was emailing blue bloody murder about the torture and named Stanford. Online common knowledge. So, they lost it. They tried to throw out the Time Tunnel while we were in it. We cut them loose and kicked them out as a result. We are not attached to them. Know that we claimed Stargate. Nasa et all, were too superior and too star struck on themselves to appreciate it. So they torture and…Viewing Surfaces …and the Pentagon released a scary tid bit and the assumption was, to us in Stargate since we use the

RNM as harmless psi link, for us to try to warn others. Hey, they have mass RNM mind control ability they can use to make an enemy obey a command'. In other words using RNM as a *weapon* on humans. Stargate recons and reports. Like the ancient *wooden walls* warning by the Oracle.

Gideon's Bible - II Chronicles   Chapter 6
6:28 "If there be dearth in the land, of there be pestilence, if there be blasting, or mildew, locusts, or **caterpiller**s; if their enemies beseige them in the cities of their land; whatsoever sore or whatsoever sickness *there be*:
…
6:40 Now, my God, let, I beseech thee, thine eyes by open, and *let* thine ears *be* attent unto the prayer *that is made* in this place.
6:41 Now therefore arise, O LORD GOD, into thy resting place, thou, and the ark of they strength: let thy priests, O LORD GOD, be clothed with salvation, and let they saints rejoice in goodness."

As for Stargate I am well aware there were others. But now is now and it was being trashed for others agenda and profit. Stargate has to be claimed to be realized or they will lose it for our culture and what it will bring in the future. Now all we wanted was to get it handled to save it from certain destruction. The other Viewers and participants who sweat blood helping with this endeavour, whose lives it was built on would agree. This Open door to the 5th D has to be saved for what it is. Our Stargate has to surface and be acknowledged to grow and strengthen and lead to its rightful conclusion of clear rapid progress. Not be stalled by some political/religious trash. It is the future of our kind, containing seeds of interstellar travel, and more. They would only keep things linear and fly around chunks of rock ....condemned eternally or for many millions of years confined to our solar system. It's just too valuable. These others in the way, are not doing anything but destroying it. Stargate has to be given to the rest of the people, to make sure trashing is not even close to happening again. The people need to know about their Stargate.

Former Military jumping; View match with rope line from out the back

Outdoor music festival in Canada, along with professional Rescuers, Kevin Costner helped also; 'The Postman'   Kevin Costner in RV of the cap

Remote Views of Yemen and off shore (below)

So, running off with the ball to give it to the rest of humanity. Pretty sure the others would not only understand they would agree if they new the full details. someday they will. I actually shared quite a bit of the pain this birth came with, as much as I could. trying to save it. Most of our youth would agree too, if they knew the truth. Claiming Stargate is necessary, it was way deep down, but there is a Meg down there now...and it has to come up. To be secured once and for all. For whatever it adds on the way forwards. With the knowledge of the ancient Egyptian Viewers too it is just too priceless. And ripe with promises of knowledge for all. That's just truth and honour and our way. Our way, our beautiful wonderful curious creative progressive happy positive culture. And it is to stay that way. I don't and won't let them keep insisting on their goofiness instead of our truth and work and this blessing on the way forwards. Stargate is the gift and heritage of our civilization. Anyone trouncing it is not only wrong or criminal they are just downright blockheads and need to be removed. If they won't, they can be left behind as this moves on and ditches them. They are inadequate if they want to play revolving dining rooms in the solar system they are free to. But they need to be cut loose publicly and not allowed to access this to ruin it. Bleep and I are not being greedy. Aside from my squawking we are more than happy to work entirely free. It is the trashing and blocking and ruin we are objecting to. That's why this is being taken from Nasa and the other politically focused. These are Quantum days, not linear. This accomplishment needs to advance. Humans need to step into the future and give our civilization its due. And it is due!! All the other Viewers can have their due credit as founding members of the original Stargate! Remote Viewing advances, it is now going forwards turning up new discoveries. I found a lone papyrus that fantastically enough, links to events concerning the Military conflict in our very own time! Stargate helps our Military in many strange and colourful ways. I typed volumes but no Star Trail is to be blazed without a lot of sheer hard work and determination. We found the keys, and that's all that counts. They can build on it to go forwards, Computers took many years from their conception. Someone gave a copy of the 'I Ching' to a mathematician. That was the seed of the idea of computers. They are a marvellous wondrous development. This is just one extension of such discovery and exploration, at the very core of our entire way of being. It is what we all live and work and learn for. The *why* of our kind. There is not a single reason any more, in our modern digital times for such secrecy. There is no safety being like this anymore. The treatment under Nasa was horrendous, the potential for abuse our worst nightmare. and they are intending more based on its secrecy. That's what they just showed me. Flaunting. Always in Power and Control. This will not be allowed to happen. We have real men and we intend to use them.//Here more from the RV info vaults of ancient Egypt. The 'capsule' shape also seems to be repeated in procession, like describing a conveyor belt. Or, looking down from above, on a 90 degree angle, the capsule shapes are also like a platform structure. The rounded shapes of the floors or platforms, are very much like what is described here. Multi levels, structures up and down as well as moving along in a linear mode.

Structure and shape descriptive, repeats coming into significance. Especially prominent visually in our times, given our city skyscrapers. The Ship the Maersk Alabama was attacked again by Pirates, fought off this time around. More on the platform structure coming into RV focus.

RV descriptives of advancement, levels, teleport? (b&w) Tomb of Ramses VI

Skyscraper with platforms, in construction; Alabama Maersk, ship levels; capsule shape; Enlargement from Tomb of Ramses VI (see above)

Discovered 'meanings' and links appearing clear to us, during a time context when the shapes and form, the structure, was relevant to concerns and events already being played out in our times. Part of the main motivation and focus of the Views seems to be *advancement* on Earth. // As for the Stargate I use the term *abscond* playfully. I took claim for all Stargate Viewers. People have no idea this is real and there are fools trashing it. Since they are not being told the truth we teamed to honk the horn, like an angel with a trumpet. Opening Stargate as a realized dream and anything it does is to be appreciated. Who knows what the next step will be it is so full of potential and promise. Stopping or blocking it would be like some ninny not wanting them to develop computers because it was 'scary' to them. Basically what censorship is, an attempt to shut down freedom and creativity. Refusing and rejecting anything not built on their own success, they are creatively selectively blocking advancement. Open Stargate is going to be fine in the long run. These are strange times, and where there were many Viewers who participated in building Stargate. For many years now, it was a secret black ops. But there is a C. Megalodon (that's a giant prehistoric shark) down there insistent on destroying it, now. Many thanks and sincere recognition to all involved. This Stargate is Open so we may dream of realizing the Star Trails. The respect of life forms requires certain ethics. Some at Nasa are lacking of them entirely for Earthlings let alone for Outer Space. We will be lucky if aliens don't commit planet wipe. Currently the space program is good for tooling around the solar system. They turned space exploration into a cess pool, literally. The toilets don't work and they crammed them in like sardines! Miserable failures, they show no spirit, no ethics; they would be thrown overboard off a ship.

The following are examples of more coded arrangements the Eyes watch for. Lately, another View theme that is showing up is the all Franken(stein), arrangement. Signalling what is on their minds in Swat, by the looks of the Chariot papyrus take on it. Times that are livid with assaults by an Anti Christ. Remote View indications urging extreme caution and warning. The reason for a Viewer's guidance is above all aimed at survival and Freedom. We don't fight on Earth to Win anything but our Freedom.

FBI inclusion as per request -photo from the Islamic Caliphate meeting held in Chicago 2009; arranged showing of the letters 'URL' (computers were being hacked).

 1. 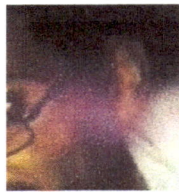 2.

1. Sample of an exposed Subliminal on the tv screen. Not sure who they thought in the law/spies business this new arrangement would be 'fooling'. 2. Sample of pink (sometimes other colors) media splotches sometimes added these days

White media inserts, matching hat outlined in dots; blue insert

Swat fighters; 'Franken(stein)' look; face slit; sample RV of bad guy bag head with eyes

   nukes on horse's forehead; slit match

'Chariot' papyrus ancient View theme visual

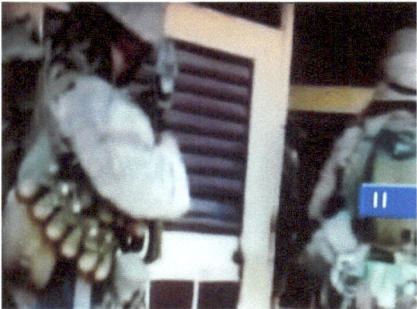

Troops Iraq '08; FBI, SS, Security forces

NY Policeman; LA Police with the Jim Carey mysterious '23' on top

'Chariot' copper top orb 'cops & robbers'; bomb scare NY Times Square; Cops on the prowl….

Special Ops Afghanistan dog, Remote View of dog, and emote of dog helper

US Military pullout of troops from cities in Iraq, 2009; Zuggernaut, Iraq

Also thanks to *Fox Cable News Network* for the great photos over the years. The mutual arrangement, they use my written daily work, to suit their own purposes. Copyright reciprocal permission; it belongs to 1st 5th First!

www.ingramcontent.com/pod-product-compliance
Lightning Source LLC
Chambersburg PA
CBHW060815270326
41930CB00002B/45

9 780981 326115